# The Sound of Silence

# The Sound of Silence

Pauline Aweto

*AuthorHouse™ UK*
*1663 Liberty Drive*
*Bloomington, IN 47403 USA*
*www.authorhouse.co.uk*
*Phone: 0800.197.4150*

© *2015 Pauline Aweto. All rights reserved.*

*No part of this book may be reproduced, stored in a retrieval system, or transmitted by any means without the written permission of the author.*

*Published by AuthorHouse 01/05/2015*

*ISBN: 978-1-5049-3520-3 (sc)*
*ISBN: 978-1-5049-3519-7 (hc)*
*ISBN: 978-1-5049-3521-0 (e)*

*Any people depicted in stock imagery provided by Thinkstock are models, and such images are being used for illustrative purposes only. Certain stock imagery © Thinkstock.*

*Because of the dynamic nature of the Internet, any web addresses or links contained in this book may have changed since publication and may no longer be valid. The views expressed in this work are solely those of the author and do not necessarily reflect the views of the publisher, and the publisher hereby disclaims any responsibility for them.*

# Chapter One

Her birth came as one piece of bad news too many.

One piece of bad news? She was born a girl. He had unquestionably been greatly hoping for a male child. Too many? This was not the first time, but it was most likely to be the last—just like all the other times. There was only one certainty for now. She had come to join the endless queue of female children, another mouth to feed from the proceeds of unemployment, lousiness, and perpetual drunkenness. Osaro's dream for a male child had been shattered for the umpteenth time. Like a skilled gambler, he had sincerely hoped that this was the rare opportunity he had long awaited. Unlike the other times, he had gone the extra mile to plan even the tiniest detail. With an existing harem of four wives who had not been women enough to produce a male child, he had thought that the only way to see his dream come true was to procure a brand-new wife.

Day after day and night after night, he painted an imaginary picture of his new bride-to-be, the chosen one, the one destined to fulfil his purpose. In the first place, she would be young enough to be one of his numerous daughters. Again, she would be a virgin, uncontaminated, undefiled and inexperienced, one that had never been tried and tested by another man. "A virgin womb can only produce the best," he thought to himself. What could be better than the long-awaited male child? He went so far as to take pains to identify the family his would-be bride would come from. Indispensably, it had to be one with a 101 per cent record of accomplishment of fabricating male children. He was in search of an ally with whom to execute an important project rather than a companion, a business partner rather than a wife. He was not simply in search of a wife, but a wife with a difference. He was not simply looking for a child, but a child with a difference, a male child—a legacy that his nine female children from his four wives could not assure him.

In order to double his chances of success, he knew he had to seek the face not just of God but also of the gods. As a traditionalist, he had always believed in the hierarchy of intermediaries with no clear distinction between the sacred and the profane. They came across to him as two sides of the same coin. In his own understanding, backed by strict adherence to culture and tradition, he knew the Supreme Being was not to be invoked for frivolities or matters not directly connected with life and death. This, of course, was the one occasion when he really felt the indispensable and unquestionable need to disturb the Creator.

As early as 6.30 a.m. on a Sunday morning he made his way to an emerging Pentecostal church in the neighbourhood. Though himself a baptised Catholic, he felt that what he was searching for was most likely to be found in a Pentecostal church. For years he had been taught to pray for the will of God to be done, but just for this one time he was bent on the contrary—to get God to do his own will, fulfil what his heart earnestly desired. This had become his reason to be or not to be. In order to obtain a new outcome, he knew it would do him no good to return to the old. This would be like "putting new wine into old wineskins," he said to himself.

As he timidly approached the church, he could hear the pastor shout at the top of his voice, "Behold I make all things new! Old things have passed away!"

"What a divine and timely revelation!" he whispered to himself with unreserved satisfaction. This was more than coincidence; it perfectly mirrored and aligned with the purpose for which he was stepping into a church building for the first time in decades. As he joined the rest of the congregation in intonating the hymn "Do Something New in My Life Today," he was even the more convinced that his prayer had been answered. This blind faith further fuelled his enthusiasm, and he suddenly found himself no longer asking but rather thanking God for having granted his only heart's desire, even before he had asked. He had forgotten to remember that he was yet to find the woman who was going to make this dream come true.

Did the pastor not speak of something new? What again could be more new and exciting than a male child? He conducted a defensive monologue with himself as he pondered. For a while he contemplated his life in a flash. In one moment he saw all his nine daughters fade away into thin air, as the old. He could not hold himself back from the wild image of the sudden new turn his life was about to take. First, he would have proven to be the man he claimed to be. A man was never a man until he reproduced himself. Then again, his name would be proudly attached to that of a male child, never to be traded in at marriage as females did. His posterity would be assured for ever. The dream of every right-thinking African man would become a reality for him.

He had to sneak quietly away from the church as the service came near to a close. He did not want to be recognised or, worse still, recruited as a new member. After all, he only came here on this never-to-be-repeated occasion for a specific purpose. From the very beginning it had been mission accomplished. He did not leave the church the same man. The one who came in was anxiously seeking a solution. The one who left had the solution, clasped with both hands, happy, bubbling, and extremely thrilled at the drastic but welcome change his life was about to take.

As he made his way home, he could not help but call at the roadside beer parlour to share his joy with a group of men, who were, for one reason or the other, drowning themselves in pints of locally brewed wine.

"You look really happy today," said one of them.

"Are you blind? Can't you see he's coming from the church?" replied another, unsolicited.

Whatever made him so happy and radiant was no longer the main issue. All that mattered were the free drinks which followed, to be credited to the jubilant, who still kept his motives to himself.

The next day, while still nursing his hangover (to be blamed not on the quantity but quality of alcohol), he had the strange feeling that his inquisition was not yet over. The sensation that had ushered him out from the church was gradually consumed and diluted by the side effects of alcohol abuse. Doubt inevitably started setting in. "Am I really going to have a male child after all? What if the pastor's message was meant for someone else and not me?"

There was only one way to find out. As quickly as he could, he made his way to the herbalist. For a while he thought he had not properly observed protocol. He ought to have consulted the gods on the lower end of the hierarchy spectrum before venturing to encounter the Supreme Being. "Better late than never," he consoled himself. Like the bird in the cage that sings out of anger, he tried to show some enthusiasm by humming a familiar song as he approached the threshold of this traditional messenger of the gods.

The herbalist was not in the least surprised by his visit. He had been expecting it for a long time. In order to make his business more sustainable, he had busied himself with the details of the needs and desires of his potential clients. He identified them more by their problems than by their proper names. For him, Osaro was the man who desperately needed a male child to counteract his reputation as "the all-women man". The herbalist knew his business all too well. He also knew that those who came to him for help only wanted to hear that there was a solution to their quest. In fact, he would not do himself any favours by proving the contrary. All he needed to do was to show that he knew the problem even before he was consulted. No one bothered to ask how he came to know. The fact that he knew was all that counted; that he knew the problem also meant that he had the solution. He would not be a herbalist if he did not have the solution to every problem great or small. The unavoidable issue, however, was the cost. Osaro had not considered this when he set out on his mission.

"You'll need to provide a white and spotless virgin he-goat and a white cock with three black spots on the head."

"What?"

"Then you're not ready to embark on your journey. You know your way out. Come back only when you have the items."

He knew he would not escape paying his dues as he had done in the church. He could not be lucky twice. He also knew what these uncommon and hard-to find items signified. He had to put a monetary value to them, and he did not welcome this idea. He had not yet borrowed the money he needed to arrange and conclude the marriage rites of his new wife. This was the only financial commitment he had envisaged. Any other business involving money would only drive his dream further away from coming true. He was fundamentally a chronic miser. He was poor and had never been significantly employed. He had piloted the affairs of his large family without any tangible job. Yet he was very calculating and prudent in spending money, especially the money he never had. He knew that this time the herbalist was being unnecessarily greedy. He was not going to allow himself to be exploited by a man who made his fortune from the misfortunes of others.

"I'll be back when I'm ready with the items."

They both knew that nothing could be farther than the truth.

Before he could proceed with making arrangements for marrying and bringing home the fifth wife, he had one more mission to accomplish. He had been through this three times before when he had to bring home the second, third, and fourth wives. What he needed now was not experience but bravery and diplomacy. He summoned all the courage in the world to gather all four wives in the same room to break the news of the arrival of a fifth. He had to do this without losing his pride and honour as a man. As the head of a polygamous family, he was convinced that he needed an ally.

His choice could not but fall on his first wife, Ese. Like the previous three times, he always counted on her. She was the love of his life. She was the one to whom he had vowed eternal fidelity, until the issue of childlessness became insurmountable. She had no option but to allow him to have his way and bring other women into the family, but deep inside she knew he did not love her enough to accommodate the predicament of their unproductiveness. Though she was a woman who married her husband out of love, she was also aware of the cultural demands to bear a male child. Though she could not give him one, she was not at the same time able to prevent him from getting one. She was determined to stand by her husband at all costs.

"You look beautiful in your new dress," muttered Osaro.

"Me?" Ese exclaimed in surprise. She had had the same dress for a while. She was fond of it, as she owned only a few dresses. Coincidentally, it was one of the few items of clothing bought for her by this same man who now sounded as if he was seeing it for the first time.

"Who else? Besides, you know you're the most beautiful woman in the whole world."

"What do you want this time?"

She knew her husband all too well. He had not been skilful enough to change this formula. He had always approached her exactly the same way whenever he wanted a favour from her. Though she had always known he would not stop at anything to get a male child, she had not expected this to happen this soon. The last wife, Queen, had been the latest wife for barely one and a half years. Queen was more beautiful than the name she bore. She was exceptionally conscious of her beauty, which made her both proud and arrogant. She was every man's dream in the village. Osaro married her because he was blinded by her beauty, only to discover that she was no more able to bear him a male child than the other women before her. However, unlike the others, Queen refused to remain in her position as the last wife. She was often rude and unruly. She refused to take her turn to cook for her husband, yet she pretended to sleep with him every night. Until he married her, Osaro never had to cope with the challenges of a polygamous home. Ese, as the first wife, played the motherly role that kept the family together in apparent unity. Queen was an exception, and her arrival brought nothing but problems and more problems. As he prepared to make his intentions known to his wives, he felt he had an additional hard nut to crack with Queen.

"Over my dead body! If you think you can bring in another woman after me, then you've got another thing coming!" Queen threatened.

"See who's talking! What goes round comes around," scoffed the second wife.

"Game over! Your reign is over! Time to hand over! You've failed in your mission!" added the third.

"It's not my fault that you couldn't prevent your husband from marrying me. As far as I'm concerned, no woman will step into this house after me. I'm the last wife, and there's no room for any other." Queen was now furious. They all knew Queen. She would stop at nothing to get what she wanted.

Ese had to take control of the situation. Osaro found himself unable to preside over this family meeting, which was gradually transforming itself into a war of women.

"Look Queen, you really have to be reasonable here," Ese insisted without success.

"Are you begging her?" The third wife was incredulous.

"Why should you?" The second wife interrupted. "She came into this family for this purpose, and, as you can see, she's no different from any of us." The third wife consoled herself. While all four wives were engaged in a verbal war of attack and defence, Osaro quietly sneaked out. He had something more important to do than having to separate his fighting wives. He detested this as a man.

"Women? Who can understand them?" he wondered. It was all Ese's fault. If she had given him a male child, he would not have had to go through all this. Life would have been different. Yet his hopelessness and regret did not prevent him from executing his strategic plan. He had to bring in the last wife, convinced that this was definitely the last time.

And so it was.

# Chapter Two

Beauty was the chosen woman of destiny. She was welcomed into the family as a new player would be welcomed into a football match in which no goal had been scored. Unlike Queen, whom he had married more for her beauty than for the messianic role of bearing a male child, Beauty was aware of the challenges before her. While Queen was beautiful and arrogant, Beauty was naturally and effortlessly beautiful, graceful, cultured, and polite. She was everything that Queen was not. She had been brought up religiously by her mother, whose only dream was to see her daughter in a one-man-one-wife relationship, whereas her father just wanted her to get married to the highest bidder. For him, a woman had to marry at some given point in time and that was the end of the story.

The arrival of Beauty was like the calm after the storm. She was as different from Queen as the light is from the darkness. They had nothing in common except that they were co-wives of the same man, who, with one after the other, had hoped to realise the dream of a male child. Beauty came to restore the failures of Queen, but Queen was not going to let go so easily.

In contrast to the other women before her, Beauty became pregnant within the first few weeks, and the great count down began. The male child was definitely on his way and could not wait to be born. Osaro was beside himself with joy and excitement. He had been in this situation before: he had not only hoped for a baby boy but had been convinced of his imminent arrival. On similar occasions in the past he had waited to hear the news and then made his way to the local beer parlour to drown his sorrow over supposedly good news turned bad. This time, however, he decided to start celebrating the good news even before it came.

"Free drinks for everyone," he declared—to the joy of everyone lucky enough to be present at this august occasion.

"Is the baby boy finally here?" inquired one man.

"Not yet, but it's only a question of minutes from now."

"Are you not counting your chickens before they're hatched?" asked another, hoping his doubt would not cost him the free drinks he had been offered. "If I were you …" he tried to continue.

"But you're not me!" Osaro cut him short.

"As I was saying before I was interrupted, if I were you, I'd wait."

"There's a fifty per cent possibility that it may be another girl." Another sarcastic voice chimed in.

"The gods forbid!" Osaro exclaimed. "Not again, not now, not ever! It has to be a boy, it must be a boy, nothing but a boy, so help me God." The feast to welcome the baby boy went on for hours without anyone paying particular attention to the passing of time. The drinks kept flowing.

"The baby! The baby!"

"Which baby?"

"What kind of stupid question is that? Of course the baby we're expecting is finally here."

"Congratulations, Osaro! You've become the proud father of a bouncing baby …"

"By the way, you didn't say whether it's a boy or girl."

"What nonsense! Are any of us here expecting anything other than a boy?"

All eyes were fixed on the messenger, as if he alone had the power to determine the fate of the moment.

"What are you waiting for?"

"When are you going to make up your mind to tell us what we have been waiting to hear?"

It then dawned on the messenger that he had only delivered half the message, the more irrelevant one, the one as good as no message at all. As he summoned the last bit of courage left in him, he needed all the strength he had to run away as fast as his heels could carry him. As he negotiated his way to the most convenient exit to get away from the exasperated army of drunken men, he knew he could not dare to raise an eyelid to meet the infuriated looks on their faces, adulterated by alcohol. They sarcastically celebrated his massive and flawless display of unprecedented stupidity.

Beauty named her daughter Joy, a name that was expressive of a dream rather than the reality.

Fifteen years later Joy had grown up to become a carbon copy of her mother, Beauty. Everything about her was unique. She was the perfect picture of a girl created on a Monday after a well-deserved rest by the Creator. Every inch of her body seemed to have been put in place like a perfect puzzle. She was indeed one of a kind, like an original painting by Picasso or Michelangelo. Her perfectly sculpted body was unrivalled and evenly distributed in an imposing five-feet stature, like a national monument that was to be unveiled and admired at exclusive events that were not meant to occur more than once every three years or more. Joy was not just beautiful. There was something else about her that made her all the more alluring. She was self-confident, a quality amplified by a full-blown self-esteem and crowned with an inexplicable quality of self-consciousness. She was exceptionally stunning, and she not only knew it but equally knew how to exploit her looks to her best advantage. As a faithful member of the ministry of Pastor Joshua, she did not have to convince anyone that she was indeed made in the image and likeness of God, in spirit and in truth. She knew she had been wired and packaged for greatness and did not need any extra effort to prove it.

She had always attracted the attention and desire of all men in the village, young and old, including Pastor Joshua himself, who had on several occasions actually betrayed himself, delivering sermons and messages underpinned by his undying lust for her. In order to keep her close to him, he had to make sure that she was involved almost in every youth activity in the ministry, so much so that the church premises became a second home for her. For Beauty, it was the better option for her daughter to spend most of the day in the company of the pastor, or at least within the church premises rather than hang around town with the crowd of jobless village champions, whose only intention was to have a taste of the national pudding that she had become.

Osaro did not hold a similar view. He seized every available opportunity to express his displeasure. As Joy stepped out one morning to make her way towards the mission house, he yelled, "Don't you have anything better to do with your time than waste away in the church in the name of serving God?"

"Like what?" Beauty broke in. She always came to the defence of her daughter, especially against her husband. She would never miss any chance in this world to give him a piece of her mind as far as her daughter was concerned.

"Something! Anything! Anywhere except the church!"

"Like going to school like every other girl of her age?"

This was a no-go area. She knew what her husband felt about women's education, but nothing would stop her from pushing her luck a bit further. He had never been known to bend the rules or change his mind once it was made up. It was not just about his opinion alone, it was about tradition. He had never believed in women's education, and it became a taboo subject after he had lost the dream of a male child. Joy was there as a constant reminder of his unfulfilled dreams and desires. She was the final nail to the coffin of a male child. She was the end of the road. She represented the death of a dream that was never meant to be resurrected again, not even on the day of resurrection itself. He prided himself as a man of tradition and considered it an absolute waste of time and resources to send any of his myriad of female children to school. He did not even contemplate sending his never-to-be-had male child to school. He was too busy focusing on his ego and the prestige a male child would mean for his posterity and position among his peers.

Although education was out of the question, the death of his dream of fathering a male child shifted his attention to the huge profit he would make for himself from the proceeds of the marriage of his daughters, whom he proudly flaunted as his "investments." He would often day dream about his prospective in-laws. His scheme was to give them away, not in any particular order of priority defined by age, but in accordance with the demands of the existing market and the specifications of the highest bidder, following the economic law of demand and supply. In displaying his daughters as goods for sale, Joy was the winning ticket, the one that was most likely to find a suitor first. The position of the first husband would determine and set the standard for future suitors. He would also be the one who would eliminate the curse of poverty from Osaro's lineage and the one who would make his name resound in the neighbourhood and beyond. It did not matter whether or not he made his daughter happy as long as the cash kept flowing. After all, happiness had nothing to do with marriage. In his mind, he could not help but think about all the things money could buy him. With money he could build a new house, buy a car, get a chieftaincy title, and buy his way to fame and prestige. This was worth far more than the much-desired male. The birth of a female child wasn't a bad idea after all, he told himself.

# Chapter Three

Pastor Joshua had been born with the dream of becoming a reverend father in the Roman Catholic Church. Rather than this being a vocation, his idea of the priesthood was to see it as a job, just like the millions of other jobs and professions out there. The only difference was that this job came with prestige, a free car, free accommodation—and to some extent, free women or at least freedom with women—without the additional hassle of sweating out a career. All he was expected to do was to make it through his diaconate and ordination to the priesthood. He was so desperate to see his dream come true that it was never to happen. He was caught cheating at the Pastoral Theology exam in his fifth year and was immediately expelled from the seminary.

Joshua was never really a bright student. He was never committed to gaining any intellectual knowledge that would enable him to fruitfully engage with the demands and rigours of a priest in the making. Although he did not possess the natural aptitude to become a priest, he had not expected the outcome of his ordeal in the seminary. He had cheated his way through primary school, and his final grades on the General Certificate of Secondary Education were generated by the first generation of computers in a local business centre. His expulsion from the seminary did not by any means end his vision. He was not intelligent, but he was definitely smart—well above the average level needed to survive in a culture of vultures. He knew what he wanted, how to get it, and where to get it. The unfortunate turn of events only meant one thing—a new strategic approach and the implementation of plan B. He was never without a plan B.

On second thoughts Joshua decided that his shameful exit from the Catholic seminary was a blessing in disguise. He had never particularly liked the idea of priestly celibacy, and that was not his only area of concern. He hated the Catholic Church's hierarchy with a passion. He knew that he stood no chance of ever becoming a bishop, with the long and endless list of candidates that would come before him, strictly in chronological order of the date of ordination. In the Pentecostal Church, on the other hand, he could declare himself the bishop and CEO of his self-made ministry. He could marry the woman of his choice and possibly have children. He could have his cake and eat it too.

For him, whether he was a priest or a pastor made no significant difference. With the option of becoming a priest completely out of the question, becoming a pastor was an inevitable choice. His training in the Catholic seminary gave him enough theological preparation to start a ministry as a fully called, qualified, and justified man of God. All that was required of him to balance the equation was his deep sense of business acumen. All he needed now was a congregation who would be hungry for the gospel of prosperity and all the goodies of the kingdom, coupled with a long list of problems awaiting miraculous solutions and divine intervention, ranging from barrenness, poverty, breakthrough, effortless promotion, exam success, and wealth and money, including all that money could buy—women, position, and prestige. He was a master planner to the core. He had a very big dream.

He also knew that every big dream has a humble beginning, but he did not want to waste his time joining an already existing ministry. This would be like the journey of the Israelites, but without the hope of final arrival at the desired destination. Establishing his own ministry was the only viable means of business. He knew the church market so well that he was aware of the need for a winning ministry name. He carefully went through the possibilities: "Winners", "Champions", "Overcomers", and "Victorious". Finally he found the ideal brand for his ministry: "Miracle Assembly Centre". Joshua was aware that the search for miracles was the ultimate reason why people go to churches. Again, he purposely avoided using the tag "church" for his ministry. As a traditional African for whom there is no relative demarcation between the sacred and the profane, he was not unaware that he had to keep his options open to every possibility. What people looked for were miracles, and where they came from did not matter at all.

The Miracle Assembly Centre was located in the neighbouring village of Agbowo in the outskirts of the Ugbowon area of Benin City. Ugbowon was host to the Ugbowon Campus of the University of Benin, whose student population was mainly made up of girls. They were the first in the line of miracle chasers. They were the ones who needed miracles to pass their exams without reading. They needed to hook and remain in the good books of a generous sugar daddy and, most importantly, they needed to make a trip to an unspecified destination in Europe in the name of hard currency. The girls from Ugbowon Campus, popularly known as "Ugbowon babes", were occasional worshippers at the Miracle Assembly Centre, but they simply refused to be recruited as permanent members of any ministry whatsoever. They dreaded being tied down by a commitment to pay regular tithes, which they saw as much too tight. "We're only students," they would claim in self-justification, "without any income." Nevertheless, the truth of the matter was that while they hid away from paying tithes and contributing to the ministry, they knew they were fully loaded, without any traceable income or means of subsistence. "Babes must survive" was a popular slogan among the girls, who traded the essence of their own souls in exchange for fashion in the name of looking good. They had been known to be church trans-migrators, as they moved from one church to the other in search of the "happening" church, the one with the out-of-this-world record of miracles.

They often came to the Miracle Assembly Centre when they were broke and had no money to throw around. They particularly avoided church events such as weddings and thanksgiving services, where they were expected to participate in different offering processions, ranging from general offering, special offering, gift offering, monthly offering, friends and family offering, student offering, young women offering, and all women offering. The list was endless.

Pastor Joshua was not always happy to see this bunch of girls at his Sunday service. Although they boosted the attendance figures, this was never reflected in the Sunday collections, even when they participated in all announced offerings. They skilfully found a way of coming with a bundle of five naira notes, so that none of them gave more than a hundred naira on a Sunday. "These girls will never change," Pastor Joshua would grumble to himself as he counted the offering of the day. He always looked forward to this, especially after sweating out sermons that focused on his members' pockets rather than their hearts. "How do they expect God to be generous to them when they are so tight-fisted? These girls are real bad news for business." He would have happily exchanged the entire Sunday proceeds for half of one of the girl's Brazilian, Mongolian, or Peruvian weaves. However, he was never the type to give up.

As he continued to fix his gaze on his miserable Sunday collection, which amounted to only a week's wage of 10,000 naira, he wondered if he could afford to date one of those Ugbowon babes. He spared himself the hassle of putting a price tag on each of the girl's outfits and came up with the approximate figure of 50,000 naira. Even a whopping collection for five Sundays, going by that day's collection, would only pay for a girl's outfit. As he grappled with the figures, he refused to allow pessimism to get the better of him. For a moment his mind drifted back to his days in the Catholic seminary and he thought about how he would have been an ordained priest by now. He would not have needed to struggle to keep body and soul together or worry about paying his personal bills. He would not have had to worry about the monumental cost of marrying and maintaining the wife of his dreams and desires. For the very first time the choice of priestly celibacy began to make some sense in terms of convenience. The short-lived journey that had catapulted him from the altar to the pulpit seemed only like a flight of stairs.

In a further struggle to allow the power of positive thinking to prevail, his mind turned to Joy. Eureka! Joy was the embodiment of the woman of his dreams. She had nothing in common with these girls who had been contaminated with materialism and exposed to everything money could buy. Compared to those girls who had fake hairs, nails, eyelashes, and padded breasts, Joy was naturally beautiful and came as an entire package as the chosen one that was destined for him.

While Joy was unknowingly being secretly groomed as the preacher's future wife, her father kept waiting for the right suitor to come and her mother kept hoping that her daughter would go to school and have a better future.

Most of the men in Joy's life either adored her like Pastor Joshua, used her like her father, or abused her like the myriad of men who seized every opportunity to try their luck with her in the undying hope of hitting the jackpot of the jewel that she had come to represent. Joy had a mind of her own and knew exactly what she wanted from life, and not simply what life was willing to offer her. She felt that she was just different and that destiny was going to restore to her what it stole from her mother. She felt she was the one to break the generational curse of womanhood. She was young and had all the time in the world to wait for the manifestation of whatever destiny had in store for her. She was a woman and only had to wait without taking any further action. At sixteen, she had lived long enough to accept the tradition that women only needed to wait for things to happen, for the right man to come, for the right opportunity to present itself, with or without education. As one of the foundation members of the Miracle Assembly Centre, she had listened so much to Pastor Joshua's preaching that she could literally repeat them word for word. She had an unwavering hope that what was promised in the Holy Book would in fact come to pass for her. She had been strategically positioned to be blessed beyond measure. Nature had been generous. The Creator was not going to prove he was wrong by way of contradiction. Even in her wildest dreams, Pastor Joshua never crossed her mind as her destined man; he was still a struggling young man, and from all indications, the situation was not going to change for a very long time to come, if it was going to change at all. His situation was comparable to that of a physician who healed others but could not heal himself. He was not the kind of man any young girl in her right-thinking mind would think of marrying. Joy was praying and waiting for an already made man. Did Pastor Joshua himself not always preach that the life of a real born-again Christian should be one without struggles? That struggling was not the portion of believers but of sinners? She believed it was only a question of time before her dream of a life without hassles, guaranteed by a heaven-ordained and destiny-sealed suitor, would come true. At the appointed time, she always thought to herself.

Joy busied herself running a low-profile salon. There was no equipment or facilities other than her raw talent as a hair braider. She had acquired this skill while growing up among girls. Her salon was located in the front yard of the family compound. It had only two small low stools, which she occasionally borrowed from her father's sitting room when he had no visitors. The salon was anything but a salon, except in name. It was more of a meeting and gathering point for school dropouts, both boys and girls. The boys came to try their luck and their latest charming tricks on the girls. They used the same changeless formula, while expecting the girls to change and fall for their well-worn antiques. The girls could not understand the boys' permanent and persistent display of stupidity. Why on earth would a guy think he would say the same thing he said to another girl and expect a different outcome? Only men would do the same thing at different times to different girls and expect a different outcome. The girls mocked the boys, while the boys kept hoping that the girls would change their minds. They not only hoped, they also believed with all the conviction of a dying man's wish. They knew that before professing love they needed the virtues of hope and, more especially, of faith. And the greatest of them all was hope, the one that never died and the one that was capable of surviving the death of both faith and love. Luck, too, was another key factor they reckoned with. Maybe luck was all they needed in order to meet the girls in a good, light-hearted, and cheerful mood. That was all they required in order to get a different answer to the same age-long question, possibly formulated the same way, using exactly the same words.

"You never know with women," one of the boys said.

"They're like the river which never remains the same," added another.

As the boys gambled with their luck, the girls were busy doing what they knew how to do best. They chatted away, building castles in the air and day dreaming about the future and all it held for them, a future which was not in any way comparable to the present. Most of their conversations were about their prospective suitors—men who were worthy enough to be called husbands, men who were not only able to meet and exceed their excessive needs and desires but also the uncountable and unimaginable needs of their families as well as their extensions.

"Miss World", as Blessing was fondly called by her friends, often dominated their conversations. As a class-three dropout from secondary school, she had nothing to envy about the imaginative skills of Danielle Steel. She was a natural dreamer with such a fertile imagination and such creativity that it seemed more than death to her to discontinue her education. But she was not the kind of person to lick her wounds. She always looked beyond the immediate and turned every seemingly negative challenge into an opportunity to be explored and exploited to her greatest benefit. Dropping out from school without engaging in anything meaningfully tangible gave her all the time to develop and perfect her imaginative skills, though these were in no way comparable to those of Joseph the dreamer in the Bible.

"The man I'll marry will kiss the very ground I step on," Miss World often boasted.

"Shine your eye, Alice in Wonderland. Where in this entire *Naija* will you find such a man?" Peace interrupted as she tried to concentrate on the braiding job they were all reluctant to complete. Peace lived up to her name in every possible way. She often sat on the fence during their routine conversations. She was the proud daughter of her mother and had been raised according to the customs and traditions that imposed male superiority. "Saint Pope John Paul II was known for kissing the ground and not stepping on women, but you'll be lucky to find a man who will only step on you without beating the daylight out of you. This is Africa—worse still, *Naija*. Any woman who's ready to go into marriage should be prepared to be beaten to death by her husband. Marriage and beating come as a package, with no option. They co-exist or co-die." Peace brought out the natural philosopher within.

"Says who?" Miss World would never miss any opportunity to inject some nuggets of knowledge into the minds of these young girls who had been brainwashed by their mothers, whom she considered the real enemies to the emancipation of women. "That was in the past when men thought they owed women as property. Things have changed now. They can no longer treat women the way they like and go free, just like that! Nowadays women no longer need their brothers to fight for them. The law is there to protect them from abusive husbands by sending them to jail where they belong."

"You know this is more of a dream that reality. You know this isn't possible, at least in this part of the world. Take my dad as an example. He always beat my mum for the slightest reason or for no reason at all. She can't report him to the police. She can't even own up to this herself. If she does, who'll take care of her and all of us?"

"You can think whatever you like, but I think your mum is to blame. Can't you see? This is why things never get to change. Something evil is done, no one condemns it, everyone ignores and condones it as business as usual, and the next thing you know, it becomes and remains the norm like a permanent scar of a wound that took too long to heal. All this must stop, and it has to stop from somewhere ... someone ... us. Let me tell you, the only way out is to get our men to kiss and worship the ground we walk on. To get them to do this, we must be able to stand up for ourselves before we stand up to them, We need to know what they know, do what they do better, go where they go, get educated like them, and get a career like them as well. If we no longer depend on them to feed us and our uncountable and unplanned-for children and if we have a place to go when they throw us out, they would definitely think twice before turning us into punching bags."

"Miss World, you never stop amazing us. Where do you get all these ideas from? Stop dreaming and come back to us in this forgotten village. Things are different here, and they will never change because they're meant never to change, at least not in our lifetime. Don't you know that you're not even allowed to have those stupid thoughts and ideas of yours? In your next life please ask God to reincarnate you in another world where women can use their brains. Here and now, we're not allowed to. We're not even allowed to think we have a brain. We can't even go to school. All we have to do is to wait and wait, hoping and praying for the right husband to come along. As long as he's rich enough, who cares about whatever else comes with the package?"

Joy hardly took part in the heated dialogue of her childhood friends. Although she would not settle for anyone less than the like of Prince Charles of England or the last King of Scotland, as portrayed in the British drama film of 2006, she felt that she needed to keep her dreams to herself, most especially as everyone expected her to marry Pastor Joshua.

Deep within, her dreams and future aspirations were never built around a man who would lift her family up from the curse and misfortune of poverty. She felt she was already a disappointment when she had turned out to be another girl—the unexpected, unwanted, and unwelcomed visitor. Now she had to prove to the entire world that she was different. She was determined to change the fate of women by changing her own fate. She wanted to be the male-female, the female-husband, the female family head, the one on whom her family could rely, not one who was simply meant to attract a husband to bear her yoke or burden. She wanted to write her own story in her own way using her own language—and differently too.

While she was gradually growing up to be the woman with a mission, she knew she had to lean exclusively on her unwavering faith in her fate as a born-again Christian, a faithful listener to the inspirational and motivational messages of Pastor Joshua, the unquestioned man of God.

# Chapter Four

Joy was so deeply engrossed in her thoughts that she did not notice the approach of her aunt Comfort, who was making her way from Benin City on a typical hot scorched afternoon. She seldom visited except, as she often said, "a matter of life and death". Comfort was a business woman to the core. She handled any deal and transaction that came under the definition of general merchandise. She was into anything that could be bought and sold—goods and services, import and export, you name it. After more than fifteen years of a childless marriage, her husband had gone ahead with two subsequent marriages and had children from both women. Despite the stigma and humiliation she had to endure, she knew the surrounding culture all too well to allow herself to be taken by surprise. She knew exactly how to make herself important as one who mattered, and she went about doing just that. She made several trips abroad annually. On her outbound journeys, she took along whatever she thought were essential commodities for her fellow nationals. She took bush meat, dried fish, and Congo meat and sold them at exorbitant prices to those hungry for a taste of the motherland. On her return journey she brought back everything and anything that women who never crossed the borders found hard to resists—fashion jewellery, original hollandaise wrappers, lace, original virgin Brazilian, Mongolian, Peruvian, Malaysian, Cambodian, and Indian hair, made in China. Her trips often lasted several months.

Her husband was more than happy to have her off his back for as long as it took. It was not easy for him to have such a cultural taboo as a wife. She was such an uncontrollable and independent woman. She behaved like one who had paid her dowry herself. She was accountable to no one, not even to herself. She had more money, influence, and power than the man who had paid the price to have her as a wife. Unlike her husband and co-wives, her numerous customers waited patiently and eagerly for her return. They had to use all their available skills and all their means to make and save extra money in order to treat themselves to the rare products that came directly from Europe. They could not wait to display their latest acquired jewellery or wrapper at the next forthcoming occasion, which had become a weekly practice. Traditional marriages, child dedication or naming, weddings, funerals, thanksgiving services, anniversaries, and birthdays—any occasion was good enough for them to arise and shine and show off.

Comfort's exact destination in Europe was unknown to everyone except herself. What she did during those long months away was a completely different issue. What mattered to her and to the people around her was that she was a rich, successful, and influential woman. She was a frequent special guest of honour at public and private functions and events, where the only language spoken and understood was the language of money, all it stood for and all it was able to do. With money, Comfort had been able to buy, redeem, and redefine her identity. She was no longer the barren woman but the "happening woman", the woman every other woman wanted to become, including women with children, who were more than happy to trade their children for the wealth and influence she displayed.

"Auntie! Auntie! Welcome, Auntie!" Joy was beside herself with excitement as she staggered from her happily interrupted daydreams.

"Joy, I can't believe you waste your life away here all day in the name of running a salon. Look, just take a very good look around. You don't even have any equipment. What kind of profit do you hope to make here if all you can do is plait and braid hair? You can't even fix ordinary weaves, because you don't have a common hair dryer. Where do you think this will lead you? The earlier you wake up from your slumber and do something about this, the better for you. I can't understand why your mother, my own sister, is allowing you to do this to yourself. I don't blame you, I blame her. She's too soft and faint-hearted. She can't even fight for herself against that good-for-nothing husband of hers. Imagine! She even feeds him and gives him money to drink himself to a stupor. What kind of woman would enslave herself to a man in this manner in this day and age? Not me!"

"Auntie, please tell Mama to convince Papa to send me to school. I want to go to school. All my mates are in school now, and that's where I want to be, and that's where I should be now, not in this salon."

"Did I hear you say school? Just listen to yourself! Let me tell you, education is no longer what it used to be. Many parents struggle to pay for their children to go to university, but things aren't exactly what they seem to be. Our universities are populated by students who shouldn't be there in the first place, who don't want to be there in the second place, and, worst of all, who don't know why they're there. Do you want me to go on? Listen, the majority of those students are there because they've bribed their way through or paid someone to write their exams for them. Didn't you hear about the strike of university lecturers? It's been going on for more than six months now. They've been fighting with the government to give them more money for research and resources, but do you think they really care? Those money-hungry businessmen and women who call themselves lecturers! They complain that students don't attend lectures anymore, yet the fault is entirely theirs. Do you expect them to waste their time going to lectures when they've been forced to buy photocopied hand-outs? Anyway, what's the point of going to lectures to hear the lecturers read out to them what they could read on their own in the comfort of a cybercafé or even a club? Those lecturers use the strike as an excuse to go off and do their own business. Some of them even travel with me to Dubai in the middle of the full academic session. What happens to the students then? Do you blame them? They roam about the streets, the girls sell their bodies to make ends meet, and the boys get recruited into kidnapping groups. Instead of using their brains to read, they prefer to use them to plan and execute all kinds of evil. Do you know why? It's all because of money. Money is the ultimate end. It's the reason why people want to get educated. But come to think of it, what is education without money? Do you know there are graduates who can't even spell their names correctly? Then again there is the problem of employment. Do you know a graduate has to wait an average of five years before getting the first job? How many graduates are taxi drivers? Do you think they went to the university to learn how to become taxi drivers? And if it's this bad for the boys, what do you expect for the girls, whom our society does not expect to be educated in the first place? Let me tell you, if you want to go somewhere or be somebody in life, you must believe me, education is no longer the key. To be honest, it's never really had been, especially for women here in *Naija*. Do you know that when women get too much education, they find it difficult to get a husband? Men are afraid of such women. They think they know too much. They think they know more than them. Men don't like women they cannot dominate and push here and there. Are you ready to go through so many years only to get the kind of education that will make you unmarketable as wife material?"

"I understand, Auntie, but I still want to go to school. I beg you, will you talk to Mama for me? Okay, if you say the government universities are a disappointment, then maybe I can go to one of those church-owned universities like the New Wine University in Okada Village?"

"There you go again! Those so-called universities owned by the so-called end-time churches are even worse. Unlike missionary education brought by the white man, which was free, Church education these days is nothing to write home about. How can a university that is being sponsored by the generous donations of its members be so unaffordable to those same members? It's like selling something I can't afford to buy. What's the point? If you believe they're in any way better or different from government-owned universities, then you would believe anything. There's not one single difference—oh, apart from the exorbitant money they charge for the same worthless degree. Their graduates go through the same ordeal to secure employment after education, except for the few who are highly connected. As far as *Naija* goes, the story's the same and can't be told differently. Oh, okay, if this isn't true, then tell me why is it that the same pastors who oversee these universities send their own children abroad? Why do you think they do this? Can't you see? They convince people that the education they provide is the best, but apparently their best is not good enough for their own children. Don't you understand? It's all part and parcel of the same money-making scheme. Some of them only admit their own members. Why? Are they some kind of secret cult? They call themselves Christians, yet they propagate the highest forms of discrimination and division. By the way, why am I wasting my precious time with you?" Comfort tried to come to a conclusion. She felt she had already said too much to the wrong ears. "Where's your mother? Let me drum some sense into her dormant brain." She made her way towards the main house.

"What a long time!" Beauty pretended she was now seeing her sister for the first time, but she had silently and secretly been listening to the conversation between her sister and her daughter. She was unsure about the right time to join in. Both parties seemed to be rightly wrong and wrongly right at the same time. She shared the dream of her daughter of going to school and eventually to the university. As a mother, she had always wanted her daughter to live a life better than hers, to have a better husband than hers, to have a career she never had, and above all to have the wealth, comfort, success, independence, and influence that Comfort had.

Beauty often thought that her sister would have been highly successful in any career. She was endowed with the astute ability to paint the picture of what was not, convince people that it was, and to make a lie to pass for the absolute truth without any objections. Her highly overdeveloped skills in persuasion made her something between an astute businesswoman and a lawyer who was obsessed only with winning, drawing exclusively on knowledge of the rules of the game and how to use them to her advantage in favour of the truth or what looked exactly like it.

"So your plan is to sit down here in this village and in this ridiculous arrangement you call a marriage and allow your daughter, your only child, to waste away just like that? What's wrong with you? What kind of mother are you? Don't you love her at all?"

Beauty knew her sister. She knew she hated being interrupted and was never known to ask one question at a time. Her questions were often just rhetorical invocations to which she never really expected answers.

"I understand why you can't stand up to your husband and take control of your own life, but it beats my imagination that you're not brave enough to stand up against him for the future of your child. Well, God knows I'd kill to secure the best future for my children. Maybe that's why I'm childless. God doesn't want me to become a murderess."

"Come on, my dear sister." Beauty tried to pull her sister into a corner and secure some privacy, away from the giggling girls whose curiosity and restlessness was gradually gathering momentum. "It's not as you think. You of all people should know that it's not easy with my husband. I keep fighting him to send Joy to school, but he refuses to reason with me. He sees her as his failure and as evidence of his inability to father a male child. I haven't given up. I'll keep pestering him as long as I have breath. Look at me! Just take a good look at me! Do you think I want my daughter to end up like me?"

"Beauty, you never cease to amaze me. What planet do you live on? I can't believe that you still harbour the dream and illusion that education's the way forward for our children. If you must know, the goalpost has moved, and this didn't happen yesterday. Today it's all about what you can buy or sell or, better still, buy *and* sell. And the only recognised intermediary is money. Even education's about buying and selling. Don't the lecturers sell their handouts? Don't the female students sell their bodies? Even the male students offer raw cash in exchange for good grades. Do you want me to continue?" No one needed to remind Beauty that Comfort's question did not require an answer. "Even the so-called churches nowadays are all about money, all it can afford and all it stands for. Believers buy and pay for prayers, anointed handkerchiefs, even anointed books, holy oil, mantles, and the like. People believe they pay God. They give money to him in exchange for more money, power, breakthroughs, promotions, and even visas to travel abroad!"

"Okay, okay!" Beauty had already heard enough of her sister's lecture to the girls before she had joined in the conversation, and she did not want a replay. "So what do you want me to do?"

"Now you are talking. You need to start laying the foundation for building Joy's future, right now, right here."

"Tell me how. I am all ears."

"There're no two ways about this. I'm sure you know what I'm driving at. All you need to do is release her to my custody, and I'll take it up from there. She has to go with me to the city, see what the city is like, and begin to build her history as a city girl. She'll work in one of my exclusive beer parlours. Only politicians and those who've got real money to spend patronise this parlour. She can make huge sums of money from tips from these honourable and much respected men. They'd do anything to invest in nature's work of art by showing appreciation. You don't need to worry. I'll be there to make sure nothing goes wrong. Oh, lest I forget, get ready to start looking forward to the end of the month like government workers do. The only difference is that you'll not have to work. You won't even need to wait until the end of the month, and you'll receive more than their meagre salaries. What do you think?"

"This sounds exciting, but are you sure those men in the city will let my daughter be? I don't want any problem. I'd rather prefer her to remain here in the village with me and wait for her destiny to manifest."

"Did I hear you say destiny? The only destiny we have is the one we work hard to create for ourselves. Stop being the lazy dreamer that you are. Only the lazy ones like you dream. In the real world people make their dreams happen."

"Okay, I have heard you. I'll speak to my husband and let you know what he thinks."

"Speak to whom? About what? That dream-killer husband of yours? I can see you haven't learnt anything about men. You and I know that he'll never support you or give his consent. He'll oppose you just to spite you and to prove that he's still the one who wears the pants in this family. He doesn't care about anyone else except himself. Look, my dear sister, if you really want this whole thing to work, then you mustn't let him know, at least not until our plan has been executed. That's the only way out. This is how men should be treated if women are to have their way. The rule is never to let them know what your real intentions are until you have done exactly what you intended to do."

After so many years of marriage, Comfort could comfortably assume the role of a marriage counsellor or pass for a motivational speaker for her skills and experience in matters relating to marriage and relationships. However, Beauty did not need her sister's persuasiveness in order to make up her mind about what she really desired for her own daughter. All she needed was right there before her, in flesh and blood. Comfort was everything she had always wanted to be and have: money, prestige, connections, independence, and above all, the right to choose and live her life precisely the way she wanted to without any feelings of guilt. She owed no one an apology or justification for just being herself.

If she had missed life's train and was not like her sister, she was all the more determined not to allow the same to be the fate of her only child. After all, Joy could become what she could not be herself. Yes, she was like a second chance to put things right. Beauty knew that her opportunity was here a second time, the last time. It was now or never.

# Chapter Five

A couple of days later Joy found herself in the early hours of a cool morning in the local motor park. All the arrangements had been secretly made by her mother and had not aroused even the slightest suspicion in her father. She had plenty of explanations to make, but this was not her priority for now. This was the very first time that Joy would be separated from her mother, but the excitement of the adventure she was about to embark on dominated her feelings. There was no room left for contrary emotions. While Beauty struggled hard to rely on her weak willpower to hold back her tears and bid her daughter goodbye, Joy could not wait to begin the journey both of destiny and to destiny.

Thirty minutes later the Toyota took off without any warning, raising the red dust that could easily be transformed into a lethal weapon for yet undiagnosed asthmatic passengers. As she left the village that she was most unlikely to see again, at least in a long while, she could not but ponder this life-changing step that was to make or break her. For the very first time she breathed in the refreshing air of freedom. She felt its inebriating hand taking over her entire being and essence like one magnetised by hypnosis. In this state of euphoria, Joy contemplated all the negative things she was leaving behind for good. Her mind went first to Pastor Joshua for no specific reason. At last she could consider herself free from the golden bondage of the imposed identity as the pastor's wife-to-be. What she felt for him was gratitude, which the man of God equated with love. She did not want to break his heart by confirming that his greatest nightmare was in fact the reality.

She had a half smile planted on her lips as thoughts of her father crossed her mind. "At longest last!" she whispered to herself. Even in her wildest dreams, she had never imagined that she would wake up one day to see the dawn of this day when her father would not be there to remind her that she was the wrong gift from God—like Father Christmas sending the wrong gift to the wrong person at Easter. She could not see the lie in believing that she was finally escaping her father's plan to get her circumcised as part of her initiation into puberty. He was fundamentally a traditional man. He believed that young girls had to be genetically mutilated as tradition demanded. He turned deaf ears to propaganda about the side effects of this age-long practice. For him, it was taboo to reason about or even question tradition. "Tradition is tradition," he often said irrevocably. Osaro was also a pragmatist. He did not care about or believe in the intrinsic values of tradition except for his own individual ideology. He wanted his daughter circumcised as a way of harnessing her imaginary waywardness and preserving her virginity until the right man came along. And with virginity as an extra premium, he was more than certain of her market value.

All this was history now, at least in the making. She felt as though she could touch the sky with a finger. Her thoughts once again drifted towards what she had firmly believed. Destiny had a plan and purpose for her. She could not believe that this same destiny, which had seemed so far away in the not-too-distant past, was gradually beginning to unfold with every step that she took. "Goodbye yesterday, welcome today!" she breathed to herself as she fell into a deep sleep amidst the chattering of the other noisy passengers.

She finally woke up from her dream, face to face with the conspicuous reality of Comfort's dream home. It had been a remarkable day with so much novelty! It was too much to take in at one time, all in one day. She never imagined that such a world existed as life in the city. Now she would experience it, see it with her own eyes, touch it with her hands, and feel it right to her bone marrow. She had never seen so many cars, too many to be counted, all in a grotesque and confusing queue called traffic. She was particularly amazed at the tall, colourful, architecturally designed buildings which reminded her of the biblical tower of Babel. In no way were they comparable with the thatched roofs and half-plastered blocks of cement of her village. Never at one time in her lifetime had she seen so many people all in one place, busy doing everything and nothing, just moving in different directions, as if going everywhere and nowhere in particular, slowly and hurriedly at the same time, as if they had every time in the world and no time at all, buying and selling, hawking, yelling, cursing, swearing, casting and binding in one single continuum of a typical *Naija* high street and market place.

Comfort's home was the most amazingly stunning and bewitching piece of art. Everything had been designed and placed in the right order as if it were the work of a goddess of perfection. The five-seat Italian-designed corner sofa was a spectacular masterpiece, with matching accessories of equally imposing side tables, lamps, Persian carpets, wallpaper, and pictures, expressive of a contemporary living room that looked in every way foreign. The chandelier, inspired by a John Lewis design, was the most intimidating piece of art that crowned the beauty and elegance of the entire ambience. For a while she thought she must be in heaven, but she could not recall any detail about her transition to the world beyond. Then again, there was Comfort, right in front of her to remind her beyond any reasonable doubt that this was in fact reality. As she fixed her eyes on the dazzling and sparkling lights emanating from the chandeliers, she was for a moment transported back to the despicable and distasteful world she had known as the only possible reality.

All of that was in her past now. She struggled to come to terms with the ravishing and delightful present. No one in his or her right senses would prefer the old to the new, the trashy to the classy, or the repugnant to the graceful. She made up her mind in an instant. There was no turning back. The future was now.

She was so engrossed in deep contemplation that she did not pay attention to the presence of two other girls, Charity and Hope. Both girls understood exactly how awed she was. They had been there before and waited patiently for her to enjoy every bit of the exciting moment, without cutting it short, like one suddenly woken up from a forbidden dream. They knew she would come around eventually. Comfort dismissed both girls with a wave of the hand and an unequivocal look that they had come to understand without further hesitation. She was a woman of business. She spoke only of business and meant every word when she did so. "Business time, blessing time" was her favourite slogan.

"Joy, we need to talk immediately." There was no time to waste in pleasantries. Joy had always known her aunt to be fast and furious about her business. Procrastination was a word that never existed in her dictionary, but this time things were rather unprecedented. "I didn't rescue you from the village and the evil plans of your good-for-nothing father to frustrate your future without an adequate alternative. I didn't save you from the frying pan only to throw you back into the fire. You must listen attentively to what I'm about to tell you, and you must trust me on this one. I'm your auntie. You know I've no child of my own and I consider you as my own child, so I can't do anything to harm you in any way."

"Yes, auntie. Mama told me that I was going to work with you in one of your beer parlours here in the city. I'm very grateful. When can I start? I can't wait to start!"

"Wait before you thank me. Plans have changed, and guess what? I've decided to send you abroad, together with Hope and Charity. You see, I can't send other people's children abroad, where it's much easier to make the kind of money that you really need to make in order to count in society, and yet leave my own blood here suffering and smiling. I know your mother would have been discouraged about the idea because of the enormous amount of money involved. You know that when people have money problems, they also find it difficult to dream big. The size of their dream is conditioned by the depth of their pockets, which are often not deep enough or have holes. All the required documents, passports, visas, and tickets are ready. All you need to do now is get yourself ready to board the flight next week."

The day had already been packed too full with all kinds of unimaginable sensations. She was completely indifferent, as if there was no more emotion left in her. She did not feel shocked, surprised, amused, excited, or even happy. She was simply numb, unable to think, feel, or respond to the bombshell that had just been dropped right in front of her. Comfort, on the other hand, could not in the least be bothered. She had seen similar reactions before. She knew that the only way forward was to continue as if nothing was the matter.

"Yes, I know you were not expecting such an absolutely pleasant surprise. Did you ever imagine that someone from your village or even family would travel abroad? If a pastor had prophesied this, you'd have thought he was hallucinating. Anyway, God's ways are infinite. You only need to thank him who always work in mysterious ways. Like I told you, you won't travel alone, and you don't need to worry about what to do when you get there. There's already a job waiting for you. You'll work as a hair dresser. I've arranged for you to work in the salon of a very good childhood friend of mine to start with. Gradually, when you begin to make the first few steps on your own, you'll begin to work for yourself and earn foreign currency. I hope you realize that we're not talking about naira here, but serious, heavy money. Even cleaners abroad earn more than our bank managers earn here. That's why travelling abroad is the best thing that could ever happen to anyone in this country who's fortunate enough to have such a unique opportunity. You should count yourself lucky. But don't worry, my dear, you'll have enough time to thank me when you start making real money in dollars, pounds, and euros."

Joy was still more than credulous. The words "abroad" and "Europe" did not strike any particular chord in her or convey any significant meaning. At that moment she did not understand this as travelling overseas, going to a strange land with people of a different colour, language, and culture, different weather, and even different food. As far as she was concerned, she had felt already catapulted from one extreme of the universe to the other when she boarded the public transport to the city in the early hours of that same day. Now another journey would not make any difference. After all, it would only get better and brighter. What mattered now was money, and lots of it—more than enough to buy anything and everything, including education and what that same education cannot bring—wealth, prestige, position, power, and recognition.

Comfort knew exactly what was needed in order to dispel every tiniest trace of doubt that still lingered in the narrowness of Joy's mind and heart. She told her about a thanksgiving service they both had to attend in a Pentecostal church to thank God for this unique blessing of open doors. Comfort was born into a practising Roman Catholic family. She remained loyal to her faith as an ardent Catholic until childlessness became a challenging problem in her marriage. She did not buy her parish priest's idea of waiting for God's time. Pentecostal churches propagated the teaching that God was timeless and that the individual had the power and mandate to change this ideological time of God to be here and now. She felt that the Catholic Church overemphasised the concept and consciousness of sin, that Catholics were saved sinners. The idea of being saved and free from past, current, and future sins as propounded by the Pentecostals was more appealing to her. She did not like the focus on morality, on good and evil, right and wrong as recurrent themes in the Sunday sermons. Such concepts did not find applications in her personal life and more especially in her business world, where the end justified the means. She could not reconcile herself with the idea of the indissolubility of marriage endorsed by the Catholic Church when even Pentecostal pastors divorced their wives and remarried without heaven ever coming crashing down. She kept migrating from one Church to the other, finding reasons to change, until she ran out of reasons and came to accept her childlessness as something that would never go away. Although she never found the solution to the problem that severed her from the faith she was born into, she had to remain in her new-found Church if only for convenience. All she needed to do was to pay her tithes and make generous donations and offerings to assure her that a blind eye was turned to her misdeeds. She was convinced that in her entire lifetime, she would have sowed enough seeds to guarantee an automatic admission through the gates of heaven.

The thanksgiving serving was held in the Christ Assembly Church. It was a mega service that was organised for the agglomeration of all satellite or smaller churches to maximise offerings and collections. The pastor in charge of this ministry had planned this event to its most minute detail, using all the business skills at his disposal as bait for the greatest harvest of the year. He left no stone unturned. He had invited guest speakers, preachers, gospel artists of the moment, entertainers, comedians, and even Nollywood Movie Stars to glamorise the occasion of a lifetime, including tried and tested people that were specially recruited to share their testimonies in an extremely convincing manner. He had meticulously assigned a role to his invited guests of honour, who came well prepared. His idea was to make the congregation have fun, forget about their sins and sorrows, and show appreciation to God by giving what they had and pledging what they were yet to have.

Members had previously been briefed on how to thank God in a proper, befitting, and substantial manner. They had been given enough time to save, earn, or even borrow enough money or to take out a loan in order to meet the demands of the thanksgiving celebration. It had been scheduled to last for at least seven hours of continuous offerings, donations, and seed sowing, amidst the unequivocal and joyful noise of thanksgiving.

The order of thanksgiving had been organised and sub-divided into categories. The first was "spiritual". Members who had received spiritual gifts in the form of leadership roles and the ability to manage responsibilities in the church came forward with their thanksgiving offerings in noticeably fat envelops. This was followed by thanksgiving for "financial" increase—business profits, the ability to win unmerited government contracts, and the material acquisition of lands, cars, and properties. This was followed by the "deliverance" category, especially deliverance from accidents, kidnappers, and robbers, thanking God specifically that they were not present in the ill-fated churches attacked by the dreaded terrorism of Boko Haram. The ministering pastor had reserved a category on "special miracles", which included the ability to gain admission into a university, possibly without sitting for an admission exam. The highlight of this category was the section on the "ability to travel abroad". It was the icing on the cake and the desire of every well-meaning member of the congregation, all of whom were ready to turn in or pledge their entire life's savings in order to sow the seed for this miracle.

The special guest speaker for this category was none other than Pastor Joshua. He had taken up this additional pastoral ministry as a motivational preacher at special occasions as a means to top up his meagre collection income from his poor village congregation. His take-home for the day depended on how well and how much he was able to persuade the gathering to turn in, both as thanksgiving offerings and as seed sowings. He had done his homework well. He knew that people who had already worked hard to travel abroad, resorting to such natural means as making successful applications, would not be willing to believe in a miracle, especially after incurring expenses on visas, tickets, and passports. His target was potential travellers, and his infallible strategy was prophecy. He prophesied that somebody's destiny was waiting abroad and that it had been signed, sealed, and delivered in the spiritual world and was only awaiting materialisation at the appropriate time. The whole congregation was in delirium as everybody wanted to be that somebody. It was the most successful category of the whole thanksgiving, as almost everyone in attendance, except those who knew the rules of the game, danced forward to sow their seeds, claim and personalise this prophesy, and wait for its manifestation.

For most of them this day was never to come. Joy seemed to be the only person in the entire congregation for whom this prophecy was real. She sat quietly and drifted into profound meditation, earnestly thanking God for having what others so much desired. She was the only one who received freely without having to pay anything in return. Unknown to Pastor Joshua, who smiled at the outcome of his eloquence, his prophesy was the end of his own dream to have and to hold the only girl that was destined to become his wife. For Comfort, it was mission accomplished. Her instincts, backed by many years of experience, never failed her. She had been to many mega thanksgiving services in the past. She knew their agenda by heart, and the certainty of the prophesy about travelling abroad was as predictable as death itself.

Joy did not have the opportunity to say goodbye to Pastor Joshua for the second and last time. Comfort had deliberately made this impossible. He had played the singular role assigned to him, and that was prophecy. Anything besides and beyond this would only produce contrary results. If there was anything that Comfort was particularly good at, it was risk analysis. She knew that it was as important to calculate risks as it was to count costs. Comfort also knew that there was one last bold step to take. This time it was to protect her investment, and there was no better time to do so than now. She was sure of how to strike the iron when it was hot. They had visited the man of God. Now it was time to visit the man of the gods of the land.

"Joy, you'll agree with me that if you didn't know that I was going to that church for the very first time, you'd not be wrong to accuse me of putting those words into the Pastor's mouth," Comfort said, trying to initiate a conversation about what they were about to do next.

"Yes, Auntie, the service was awesome. I enjoyed every bit of it. I've no doubt that God spoke to me directly through Pastor Joshua. It's not as if I had any doubts, but now that I believe that everything had been planned and ordained by God, who am I to say no to this singular privilege? I'm really lucky. I've always known that he had great plans for me, but this definitely is far beyond my expectations."

"You're right, my dear, but we still need to visit another man of God. This one is a little bit different from the one we've just heard."

"Auntie, I don't understand. We already have the prophecy, and that's enough for me. Why do we need to hear from another pastor?"

"There are so many things that you still need to know and understand about God himself and the way he handles the affairs of men in this world." Joy knew her auntie well. She did not bother to interrupt her, knowing fully well that she would only come to a pause when she had emptied her basket of wild ideas. "Do you know that the God we worship as Christians is a foreign God, brought to us from a strange land?" Comfort did not wait for an answer. Joy knew that for her, questions and statements of facts were two sides of the same coin. "Now, before God happened to us, we had our own way of reaching out to him through a hierarchy of spiritual beings and messengers.

They're not very different from pastors and priests. They're all mediators, and the only difference is that they take a different route and use a different language, but they all lead to the same God. One big difference is that our ancestors and forefathers were very comfortable with them, so much so that they rejected the new way of relating to the same God through Christianity, which they saw as the new religion. But do you know what? What our people tend to reject as religion, they accept and practise in the name of culture. Don't you know that some Christians engage in practising both male and female circumcision? Did the Bible say women should be circumcised? If it didn't say so, where do Christians get this from? It's from culture. You see, Christians still pour libations and present cola nuts according to traditional and cultural prescriptions. They even take chieftaincy titles, make oaths, swear, and even belong to secret cults and societies. They become traditional rulers and custodians of some traditional practices that aren't compatible with Christian beliefs, yet they occupy the first seats in the churches. Let me tell you, in this part of the world you'll do yourself some good if you understand that religion and culture are one and the same thing."

Joy had no doubt that Comfort was right. At once her mind went back to her father, Osaro. He was a traditional man who hung in the balance between his traditional beliefs and practices and his religious beliefs as a baptised Christian under the Roman Catholic denomination. He had told his daughter about his visits, both to the church and to the gods of the land when he was looking for a male child. He did indeed believe that his visit to the messenger of the gods, especially his inability to make the required sacrifice, was mainly responsible for the outcome of his ultimate search. Osaro knew enough to believe that nothing was entirely free of charge. Everything had a price. His traditional religion and culture bore him ample witness. He became all the more suspicious of the attitude of the Catholic Church that promoted voluntary offering. He considered the option of the Pentecostals as nothing short of gambling. The pastors did name a price, but there was no correlating guarantee of the desired outcome, as terms and conditions always applied. He considered the operative mode of his traditional religion as the most applicable to his life and experience as a man. He had lived in a culture that permitted a peaceful co-existence between the God of Christianity and the gods of the land. While the gods of the land made no specific demands in terms of loyalty or wholehearted dedication, the Christian God considered to be a jealous God, had continued to tolerate the double dealings of his people. While the latter gave too much time to the back-slider to repent and be forgiven, the gods of the land were unforgiving and merciless. While the Christian God allowed his people to confess and live, the gods of the land resorted to confession only as a prelude to immediate death, without waiting until the end of time. With the gods of the land, people named and shamed the enemy, deciding whether to deform him, defame him, make him poor, or strike him with blindness, madness, or even perpetual barrenness and generational poverty.

Comfort was still making meticulous efforts to establish the continuum between the God of Christianity and the gods of the land, when she swiftly swerved and turned her Mercedes Jeep from the main road into an unpaved and dusty road. She came to a halt at the extreme end of the road and stopped in front of an unusually imposing building that stood right in the middle like a dead end. The freshly painted and hurriedly appended signpost read "Barrister Bright and Brothers: Solicitors and Property Consultants". The door to the building was left ajar as if the occupant was expecting a visitor. Both women made their way in and immediately found themselves in an exceptionally large lounge. On the wall hung certificates from different universities in Europe and America in different languages, including Italian, German, and Spanish. In another corner of the large underutilised space were trophies of all sizes in bronze, silver, and gold, all rigorously displayed in a row that looked more like a collection of trophies that had been bought rather than won.

The man sitting behind the desk in another corner of the lounge could not have won them all, even if he had lived twice his age. He was in his late forties and was dressed in a double-breasted suit in the scorching heat of the afternoon like most of the pastors they had seen at the thanksgiving service. He looked every inch like a seasoned Oxford or Cambridge professor, except for the dark sunglasses hanging on the tip of his nose as if he did not want to be recognised even in his own office. He invited both women to sit in the two empty seats in front of him. He gave the impression that he was a very busy man even on a Sunday and seemed to want to conclude their visit in a hurry. He was as professional as Comfort. Like her, he went straight to the point. Unlike her, he did not waste much time about this, using too many words when a few would suffice. He had been paid beforehand for his service. All he had to do was to deliver, and quickly too. Although the original impression was that their visit was intentional and had been pre-arranged, the barrister acted as if it was both informal and unplanned.

"Your auntie here is my business partner. She told me you'll be travelling abroad soon, so I just wanted to see you and let you know how fortunate you are. Not everyone who dreams of travelling abroad ever gets the chance to do so. I'm sure you'll agree with me."

"Yes, sir."

"Barrister Bright. Call me Barrister Bright."

"Yes, Barrister Bright."

"Without wasting too much of your time, I just wanted to let you know that your auntie has done a whole lot to sponsor your trip. I hope you'll show appreciation in due course."

"Yes, Barrister."

"Now," continued Barrister Bright, indicating a narrow door at one side of the sitting area, "go in there and in the secrecy of your heart make a solemn promise that you'll never disobey your auntie and that you're ready to do whatever it takes to return the favour she's now offering you. You'll find a pot in the middle of the room. It contains anointed oil which I got from my church. Use it to make the sign of the cross on your chest. Then close your eyes and make the pledge. That's all."

Nothing could be simpler, Joy thought to herself. It was not as bad as she had thought. At least she was not in a traditional shrine that evoked mystery, fear, and trembling. She was glad that she was not there to contradict all that she stood for as a born-again Christian. Everything in that environment looked and sounded homely and familiar—the private prayer room, the anointed oil, and then the sign of the cross. Her father had in the past reassured her that the only thing the devil could not do was the sign of the cross. Nothing was peculiar or suggested anything contrary to her belief and practice. She went through the red curtain and did exactly as she had been told. Only Barrister Bright and Comfort understood the weight and strength of what had just happened. If Joy had the slightest idea that she had just sold her soul to the devil and at no extra cost, she would have given her own life in exchange for such an invitation to dine with the most dreaded enemy.

Only a couple of days later the girls were ready to embark on their journey of a lifetime, with all its promising surprises and juicy promises. Joy's journey companions were Charity and Hope, the same two girls she had met when she first set her foot in the mesmerising home of Comfort. Since then the three girls had not had a chance to meet or get to know each other better. Comfort had taken care of every little detail in order to ensure that they never became familiar with each other or their mission. She had coached them separately, told them different things at different times, and used different language and anecdotes without raising their suspicion. She was always in control, and the only way of exerting this was to make sure they did not have the same information on which to dwell when idleness, fear, or suspicion stepped in. Nevertheless, here they were together, ready to challenge their destiny and re-write their own story by going on the adventure of a lifetime as complete strangers, ready to dare a destination yet unknown.

Charity came across as a very confident and resilient young woman, who was ready to do whatever it took to get what she wanted. At twenty-five years of age, she had absolutely nothing to envy about anyone who was seven years younger. Until that moment, she had, in her short life, seen and done more than her age could accommodate. Her greatest strength was her perfectly and athletically sculptured body that was the equal of any top model, dead or alive. Her beauty, however, was not entirely flawless. By an act of divine injustice, she was not endowed with a beautiful face to complement her great body. It was as if she was deliberately given the face of another. She was a vivid confirmation that no one was perfect. She was also as proud as a peacock. Over time she had perfected her defence mechanism. She supplemented what nature could not complement with an impeccable sense of femininity. She possessed the type of rare feminine expressiveness that could win her the Miss World crown. She had a very charming and seductive personality hiding behind the veil of a face that was unfair to her body. Charity believed that she had everything she needed in order to achieve whatever she wanted in life and from life. She had dropped out of secondary school as she was not a particularly keen learner. For her, it was always a question of trade by barter. Unfortunately, this did not always work for her.

Her parents were happy when she came home one day with the exciting news of having gained admission into the university. For four consecutive years, Charity lived the life of a true university undergraduate. She even had university accommodation on campus where her mother visited her several times. She was regularly enrolled into hundred levels in Business Management. She received tuition fees from both parents, who worked very hard to see her graduate. She had a university student identity card and even campaigned for and won the position of students' welfare officer in the university student union. Charity went as far as sitting for and passing all recommended courses and exams. But she was not, in actual fact, enrolled as a student, at least not officially. The habit could not make the monk, not even in her case.

Her mother, Patience, got the surprise of her life on the day she had so much looked forward to as her daughter's graduation. Unknown to her, Charity was not matriculated, and the journey to the graduate world had never really begun. Patience turned up unannounced with an entourage of her most intimate friends and associates to witness the event of a lifetime, which it really would have been, except that it wasn't. She had planned how the day was to be celebrated in grand style. She had carefully chosen the group's attire and accessories from the wide range of Comfort's supply from her last trip to Dubai. Apart from saving face at what turned out to be the most embarrassing day of her life, Patience was more concerned about counting her financial investment and subsequent loss. She was not the kind of woman to sweep things under the carpet and bury her head in utter shame. She was determined to make an even greater profit from the fiasco of her daughter's graduation that was never to be.

Patience was not unmindful that the type of financial facelift that she so very desperately needed could only become a reality in a faraway land. She made an initial attempt to send Charity abroad after she had sold the only piece of land that her late husband had left her as an inheritance. Unfortunately for both women, this project was never meant to see the light of the day. Charity had boarded a flight in Lagos headed for Torino, in Italy but stopping in Amsterdam. When she was stopped by immigration officials as she unknowingly tried to cross the border into Netherlands without a transit visa, her wit and charms failed her for the very first time. Up till then she had never tried to use them in an environment that was both unfamiliar and unfriendly like the immigration border. She was finally deported after three days of active and direct questioning and thorough investigation. At the end of it all, she was like someone who saw the Promised Land from afar without setting her foot on it. Those three days spent in transit seemed heavenly to Charity. It was like waking up in the middle of a dream where she was about to be crowned as the legally wedded wife of Prince Williams of Wales. That was another business gone badly, but not badly enough for mother and daughter to give up the dream of a generation. It was too late for that. The journey was one way, without return. All they had to do was to wait for another opportunity to come knocking. It finally did.

Hope was not as confident, daunting, or courageous as Charity. Unlike her, she was timid, reserved to a fault, fearful, and above all lacking a mind of her own. Others had taken every decision for her in the past, especially her imposing and intimidating mother, Precious. Although Hope never knew her father, she was constantly blamed and punished for being the cause of his death. At his demise, caused by excessive alcohol abuse due to joblessness, Precious was the prime suspect. The entire neighbourhood unanimously believed that she had killed her husband for no apparent reason other than to gain the freedom to grace the beds of other men, who were in no better condition than her late husband. In order to prove her innocence, she had been subjected to all kinds of unimaginable, abominable, humiliating, repulsive, and dehumanizing practices. She was made to drink the bath water from her late husband's corpse. As might have been expected, she was unable to prove her innocence. The nauseating smell and disgusting taste of the water provoked her to vomit and induced instant premature labour. The entire village left her to have her baby alone in utter shame and segregation. She became an outcast in a village that judged her and found her guilty of a crime she never committed. Her only companion was her daughter, Hope, on whom she turned all the ill-treatment she received, but from whom she could not be separated.

As soon as her daughter came of age, she did not mince words in making her understand her responsibility as the bread winner of the family, since she was the sole cause of the passing of her husband. Hope had been sent to Rivers State to work as a household help. She had to battle with the advances of an unscrupulous master, who was not man enough to ask his wife to satisfy his sexual urges. He used his position of authority to fully exploit Hope's vulnerability. He made empty promises about sending her to school and improving her prospects, but all to no avail. Hope was sent from his house in disgrace when his long-suspecting wife had enough incriminating evidence to put her through the doors. She found herself in Jos in Northern Nigeria, where she was subjected to the same nightmare of the overbearing husband of a woman he had no control over. The riots and religious unrests in the city of Jos came as a blessing in disguise and a reason to escape without further justification. Hope was back to the same place she had started from, without anything substantial to show for the passage of time. She had spent five years as a housemaid and a sex mate, but she was worse off than she was when she had set out.

Precious, was not the type to give up so easily. She wished her daughter had been killed in the riots and did not hide her disappointment over the survival of her only child. She had only returned to remind her of her woes as a woman, wife, and mother. It was always and only a question of time before she found the ultimate solution to the problem she called a daughter. No city in the entire wide world was big enough to accommodate them both. While waiting for the opportunity she knew would inevitably come, she engaged the services of Hope in running her evening palm-wine spot. Most of her customers were men. At the end of the working day they were not in a hurry to return to their nagging wives with their unnecessary demands and endless battles for one reason or another. Precious's spot had become an indispensable point of transit for these men. She made sure that she kept them there as long as they kept their orders of palm wine and pepper soup rolling. Precious was not as astute in business as was Comfort, who knew exactly how to count the costs before counting her profits. On the contrary, she counted everything as profit. She did not bother to think whether it was worth the while to trade her daughter for a few extra bottles of palm wine. Oftentimes, these men came, just to have their piece of her. They touched her, making compromising compliments and unfulfillable promises. Those who were lucky enough to have had enough drinks from the local brewery would lie down with her in the small back room, which was meant to be the store room, at no additional cost other than the guarantee as regular customers that they would not fail to return the next day. The bait was more than the catch, but this was a non-issue as far as Precious was concerned. She patiently waited for the day when her childhood friend Comfort would ask to sponsor Hope to Europe. She knew her friend and her line of business well enough. She belonged to that small circle of Comfort's intimate friends who knew that she trafficked girls to Europe for prostitution. Her daughter Hope had no reason to be considered an exception to the rule. After all, what is good for the goose is good for the gander, she often consoled herself in self-justification.

# Chapter Six

As the three girls boarded the first morning coach from Benin City to Lagos, they remained buried in their thoughts, dreams, and aspirations. They still could not break the ice that kept them apart. Comfort had put this trio together strategically to ensure they did not share their worries or even think of a change of mind. The confidence of Charity and the faith of Joy were enough to drag along Hope, the fence-sitter. The journey, which lasted about six hours, was over even before they knew it. They found themselves in the chaotic city of Lagos and the recklessness of its *keke napep* drivers. They were too excited about this unique city and all the contradictions it represented.

They made their way through the endless traffic and city smog to Muritala Mohammed Airport. Waiting for them at the departure hall was Barrister Bright. The girls had met him separately in Benin City as the traditional man of god, who assumed the role and function of a barrister. They had taken an oath in a small prayer room upon his instruction. What on earth was he doing there? They wondered but dared not to question. Their doubt was soon replaced by the overwhelming excitement of seeing a familiar face from Benin City here in the no man's land of Lagos.

"Good to see you again, girls. Did you enjoy your trip?" Barrister Bright was not the man to wait for his questions to be answered. The girls had come to know this about him after just one singular encounter. They smiled in unison as if they had previously agreed to do so. That was a good sign for him, a confirmation that his assignment was going to be as easy as eating a piece of cake. He had been in this situation before. He knew that girls who asked too many questions were a headache. All they were expected to do was to remain silent with a smile planted on their faces like kids who had just seen Santa Claus. "Yes girls, all is set. I've got your passports and will travel with you to your next point of call just to make sure everything goes according to plan. You've all been instructed by Comfort, I suppose."

"Yes, sir," came another answer in chorus.

"Barrister Bright, young ladies. Call me Barrister Bright. We're now heading towards the immigration border. Please, please, please leave all the questions for me to answer. Those people can be very suspicious of anyone travelling abroad. You can't blame them. It's not easy for them to be at the border watching people travelling abroad yet unable to do so themselves, so they try to frustrate lucky travellers by asking unnecessary questions and making silly demands. For them it's business as well. They make money from travellers by begging them to leave their last naira notes behind as a last resort after they have failed in their extortion plans. What's even the more vexing is that they see problems where they don't exist. Free transit is no longer the option, they'll definitely find something to destabilise you and make you want to pay any amount just to be done and dusted with them. It's more difficult to cross a Nigerian border with legal travel documents than to cross any other border in the world, even with illegal documents. So, girls, silence is the watchword here. Say nothing and we'll sail through no time. Say something, and that's the end of the road not just for you but for everyone else as well."

Everything went exactly the way Barrister Bright had envisaged. Comfort had her men at immigration. No further questions were asked. They had been on her regular payroll, with extra tips for every successful trip.

The girls had been through an emotional roller coaster. Within the last few days they had to handle many new situations, but none was comparable to the excitement of boarding a plane for the very first time. They hardly even had the time to savour all the in-flight entertainment and selection of refreshments. They never even came to terms with the once-in-a-lifetime experience of taking off. Before they knew it, it was landing time. For the first time they knew where they were destined: Niamey, the capital city of the Democratic Republic of Niger.

Upon arrival, they were met by a rather tall and slim middle-aged man. He simply introduced himself as Musa, without observing further protocols. Everything about him, except his dark sunglasses, was a pointer to his religion as a Sunni Muslim.

"Girls, my assignment ends here," said Barrister Bright. "I have a return flight to catch in the next hour or so. This is Musa's terrain. From this point on he's replacing me as your guide. One thing though. The rules remain the same, but this time around you don't even need to wear a fake smile. All you've got to do is pretend to be invisible and follow instructions. Everything'll go according to plan and you'll be in Europe soon. Musa here will explain further."

Plan? With this unbeliever? Joy did not dare to show any emotion that would contradict her countenance. She had never had any doubts about this journey until now. Her steadfast faith in the divine plan and purpose for a bright and prosperous future would definitely have nothing to do with a Muslim, with one who casually accepts Jesus as a prophet and nothing more. Charity was unperturbed. It was not part of her character to lose focus. She was not shaken by the mere sight of a different kind of man, dressed differently, with different religious beliefs and values. She was not a practising Christian or a born-again Christian like Joy. Hope was as unworried and unsympathetic as Charity, but for different reasons. She had lived in Jos. She was very well acquainted with men like Musa.

In the meantime he had flagged down an unofficial taxi. They headed for a glorified three-star hotel in the outskirts of the city of Niamey. He instructed the girls to wait for further instructions from him, but then he never showed up again until two weeks had elapsed.

"I've been very busy, girls, making adequate arrangement for the next phase of your transfer. I'll come back and fetch you as soon as things are finalised."

Musa was not a man of many words. He often used only the words that were necessary to make his point, and he would rather not say anything at all if he had the choice. He was very hard-hearted about other people's feelings. He believed that whatever had to be done, just had to be done without apology. He had no sympathy whatsoever for a bunch of infidels in a country where the majority were Muslims. By the time Musa returned, two more weeks had gone by. He dropped off a bag of clothes and asked them to change as quickly as they could and meet him downstairs without further delay. He did not go the extra mile to explain what the clothes were for, why they had to disguise themselves, and, most importantly, how to put them on.

Only Hope was vaguely familiar with the contents of the bag Musa had left them. Both Charity and Joy were stunned. The clothes might as well have fallen from the sky. They could make no sense of the bag sitting right in front of them in the middle of the room.

"My Madame in Jos used to wear clothes like these ones. I think they call them *jihab* and *chador*. *Jihab* is like a head scarf or veil won by reverend sisters, the *chador* is like a long kaftan that women wear to cover their entire body from head to toe as a sign of modesty to prevent other men from admiring their beauty or desiring them. Women who wear these clothes do so only when they're out in public. In private they can expose their beauty to their husbands, fathers, fathers-in-law, sons, stepsons, brothers, nephews, or other women and even small children who have no concept or sense of shame."

"I won't ever wear those clothes, no matter how modest they make me look. I'm a Christian, a born-again Christian. I can't be one thing and pretend to be another. It's called hypocrisy." Joy said.

"If your plan is to frustrate our journey, then you must think again. I, Charity, am ready for anything by force or by fire. Hope, please help us to get dressed and get out of here!"

Musa was waiting impatiently. He wondered what had taken the girls so long to put on outfits as simple as a *chador* or a *jihab*. "Now, girls, all is set. You must listen to me and listen very carefully. I'm not going to repeat myself or answer questions. My duty is to accompany you to the border, where other persons will take over from me. This is all I've been asked to do. We leave tonight. The journey will take approximately three hours by road. All this while I've been monitoring the road to make sure it's clear and free from control and check points. Now everything is okay. It's safe for us to leave now!"

Joy did not know what to think, feel, or believe anymore. She could not understand why they had not taken a direct flight in the first place. She questioned why they had already spent close to one month but were still at the tooting stage of their journey. They had not even left the African continent. What other surprises would be lurking around the corner? She knew she would never get an answer to her maddening questions. She knew she had to be brave. If she ever had faith as she had always claimed, there was no better time to prove it than now.

At the border of Niger the girls were handed over to two men, who brusquely introduced themselves as the Colonel and Mohammad. Both men were not in any way different from Musa, who was more intimidating for his silence than for his utterances, The Colonel appeared to be more charming and approachable than Mohammad and Musa. They had been in the same business for so long that they knew their part well and played it to the best of their ability. Like Barrister Bright, who had left without exchanging pleasantries or saying goodbye, Musa's sudden disappearance, as if from a stage, after introducing the Colonel and Mohammad did not in any way come as a surprise to the girls. They were rather relieved, taking a deep breath as his slim but spiteful figure faded from their presence.

The Colonel and Mohammad accompanied the three girls to an isolated but open camp. There were a handful of segregated camps scattered here and there in no particular order or sequence, displaying a lack of prior planning. Each girl was to occupy a single tent without the possibility of interacting with the others except during communal exercises, such as drills on how to cross the Sahara desert. After they had been introduced to their individual tents, it became clear to the girls that while the Colonel was in charge of logistics and their overall welfare, Mohammad was concerned with practical operations, handling the day-to-day material and physical needs of the girls.

The next day the girls were gathered for the first time to receive instructions on what to do to make their journey a smooth one. The Colonel addressed them.

"Look, girls, this might be your first time, but it's not ours. You'll do yourself a big favour if you simply obey the rules and follow instructions without asking silly questions. The less you know, the better for you. All you need to know now is that you're on track to travel to Europe, but we can't guarantee when that's going to happen. If you're lucky enough, it might be a question of weeks, but it might be months or even years depending on factors beyond our control. You need to relax and make yourselves comfortable, and before you know it, it'll all be over. Mohammad and I are here to take care of you, but only if you comply and collaborate with us. All we ask of you is obedience and docility. Let me remind you that you'll have to pay for everything you need. This is protocol. We can't accept your naira, but if you have dollars, euros, or pounds sterling, that'll be just fine. One last thing. Don't worry if you don't have any money at all. We do accept payments in kind as well."

"What!" yelled Joy as Charity covered her mouth with one hand, trying to prevent her from saying anything that would further complicate their situation.

"I'll explain to you later!" Charity assured her.

But the girls never had the privacy they needed to clarify things any further.

# Chapter Seven

During the next three months they tried several times to cross the border without success. They faced the situation, using various survival strategies to keep the dream of a better tomorrow alive.

Charity just got along. She accepted every situation with a positive philosophy. She knew she needed an ally, and the Colonel was her winning ticket. He did all he could do within the limits of his power and influence to meet her every need in exchange for the only thing she could afford to offer him, the only thing that really mattered to him when it came to a relationship with women. Charity could not be troubled about any moral judgement. She had slept with different men in the past for different reasons. She had slept with her university lecturers for a pass mark in a subject she knew everything about. This time it was survival sex, and she was fine with it.

Hope was not as smart and calculating as Charity. She soon became pregnant without knowing who was responsible. She was the rape target for both the Colonel and Mohammad, who took it in turns to secretly sneak into her tent at will. They knew she did not have the willpower to say no.

Joy, on the other hand, made up her mind to do everything possible not to be defiled by these men. They seemed more like kidnappers than protectors to her. She went without food and drink for two weeks. The men both knew it could not last longer than that; it was only a question of time before she gave in. They were too familiar with her type. They had met girls who vowed to protect their virginity but later begged for it to be taken away in exchange for a pot of porridge.

The long-awaited day finally came like an unexpected thief. The girls received the good news that it was time to proceed. Nevertheless, their joy was short lived after the Colonel's announcement.

"You can consider today as the best or the worst day of your life, depending on how you take it. If you're positive minded, as I think you should be, you'd be happy that you're gradually making progress towards your final destination. I don't intend to cut your excitement short, but you need to know exactly what to expect so there're no surprises. Let me put it across to you immediately that if you want to change your mind and return to where you're coming from, this is the time to do so, otherwise you're in. After this evening there'll be no more option to go back." He paused as if he wanted to give the girls the opportunity to decide whether or not to proceed. He had no doubt that, in spite of their fears and anxieties, none would dare to even think of defying him. He continued as one who had their consensus. "Good girls. I didn't expect any of you to go back home at this point. You've not disappointed yourselves and me. You've made a wise decision. This journey is for grown-ups and mature women, not toddlers. If you think you've seen anything yet, you'd better pinch yourselves and wake up from your deep slumber. What you've been through so far is nothing compared to what is yet to come." The girls had the impression that they had to allow him to continue without interrupting him. Their hearts were beating at the speed of a Ferrari on a racecourse. "Christmas, yes, you Christians call it Christmas. Your journey so far has been like Christmas—all fun, excitement, gifts, comfort, relaxation, and joy. You've been in a fattening room like a bride being fattened before going to her matrimonial home. Do you know why people do this? It's because they don't know what to expect in the husband's house. It's to prepare the bride for future hunger and all that will be lacking in the marriage." The Colonel was not expecting any reaction from the girls. He could feel that they were anxious about getting the details of what awaited them. "Let me put it this way. You're Christians and you're quite familiar with what your Bible says about the journey of the Israelites, lasting for forty years in the wilderness. Yours may not last exactly for forty years, but I can assure you there'll be no manna from heaven this time around. You'll have to go through all the hardship associated with living and wandering in the desert, for who knows how long, without food or water. You'll have to feed on your own body wastes or even those of others or the carcasses of strange animals if necessary. You must do whatever it takes to survive at all costs, otherwise you'll die of starvation, and that'll be the end, apologies to no one. Your parents might think you're still alive, not knowing you've been dead and unburied in an unknown land without a name or identity, not even a grave with the inscription 'the unknown hero' You're really never a hero until you've reached your final destination. You're greater fools than I thought if you think your only challenges will be hunger and thirst. Add sleeplessness. You'll constantly need to take shelter from the stray bullets of border officials who are on the lookout for migrants who trespass illegally. They'll gun you down without even stopping to think if they spot you trying to escape. If you're caught, you'll be put in prison and you'll be sure to receive the slowest and most painful death and afterwards your entire body will be systematically dismembered into pieces."

The Colonel knew that he had driven a sufficient dose of fear into the girls to get them to cooperate. He dismissed them and ordered them to be up at three o'clock the next morning.

Joy was utterly without words as she lay on the floor of her tent. She could not believe that her journey of destiny had become her worse nightmare. She could not understand what and where things had gone wrong. Could Comfort have been part of all these? Was this the evil plan her mother agreed to? And Pastor Joshua? Was this the miracle he prophesied? Joy knew that thoughts about her past would only bring her sorrow and regret and that going back was not an alternative for now, not after the revelations of the Colonel. Her *via crucis* must begin in a question of hours. She must be ready to embrace it. In her confused state of mind, she could not find the courage to pray or fall back on the reassurance that only faith could bring her. How could God listen to her now? Was he even in this foreign land with their foreign gods? Could he listen to the prayers of a born-again Christian who had literally taken on the identity of a Muslim? Who should she call on now, God or Allah? Her only viable alternative for now was to turn to the gods of her father. They imposed no limitations, and there were no applicable terms and conditions.

A couple of months later the girls finally found themselves at the Libyan border. It had been an excruciating, nerve-racking, and mind-boggling journey. It could never in any way be compared with the picture the Colonel had painted earlier. It did not come as a surprise that the assignment of Mohammad and the Colonel was soon to come to an end. In spite of everything, they were happy that the desert saga was finally history. Whatever lay ahead could not be worse than what they just left behind. Unlike the journey from Lagos to Niamey in Niger, when they were accompanied by Barrister Bright, and thereafter between Niger and the borders of Libya accompanied by Mohammed and the Colonel, the girls had to proceed to their final destination unaccompanied. They had no money to meet their immediate needs. They were in a strange land with a foreign culture, language, and religion. Their greatest challenge was that they had no one to turn to as a guide, a familiar face, or an intermediary.

"Look girls, we can't give up now. I, for one, won't—not after all we've endured to come this far and this close to our final destination." Charity's determination was the link between their present predicament and the future ahead. She knew she had to be in control. Joy's faith had begun to fail, and Hope's indifference was nothing to go by; her defence mechanism had always been denial, and it worked for her to the extent that she had even forgotten about the life that was gradually growing inside of her. "Yes," Charity continued, with the commanding tone of one who had learned too quickly in the company of the militant and ruthless Colonel, "we can't remain here. This wasn't where we set out for when we left home. There's still more journey ahead, probably worse, but the fact remains that we must be on the move, and the sooner, the better."

If Charity had any innate ability, it was strategic thinking and planning when things appeared to get out of hand. It was the right time for her to put on her thinking cap. She had survived worse situations in life. She had been deported from Amsterdam when she was just miles away from accomplishing her dream. The momentum she had gathered from this seemingly negative outcome was all she needed now to propel her to her desired goal. Finding food was not at the top of her to-do list. She desperately had to find somebody who would show them how to get out of their self-imposed exile. They needed someone who would speak their same language. Fortunately for them, they did not have to wait for too long before their unspoken prayers were answered.

Faith had lived on the streets and borders of Tripoli for a third of her twenty-one years. Her disarming ticket was her virginity and her young age. At fourteen, she had been targeted for an exclusive client in Italy, with tastes beyond those of mere mortals. He had promised the sum of 80,000 euros just for a night with an undefiled maiden. Faith had to go through the ordeal of crossing many countries, just like Joy, Charity, and Hope. She had given up on crossing the border to Europe after several failed attempts. Only 600 miles stood between her and Europe. She had learnt the tricks of surviving in a hostile environment where her closest ally was death itself. She had settled down to making profits from the business of her precarious situation. The three girls were so relieved when they finally spotted a familiar face. For Faith, familiarity was to be kept at arm's length if business was to be the focus. This was an opportunity she did not intend to pass her by. All she had to do now was to repeat the same cliché she had used in similar situations.

"So how may I help you?" She knew their situation well enough but wanted to sound both professional and distant.

"We want to know how to get out of this place. We can't remain here, and we've got jobs waiting for us to start over there as soon as we arrive. We've already spent some months in transit, and we're neither here nor there." Charity sounded both brave and reassured now that she thought help was finally at hand.

"That's no problem, but you've to listen to what I've got to tell you first." Her main persuasive strategy was her own personal odyssey and her inability to leave Libya in seven years. She emphasised her worst experiences over the past seven years in order to make them feel that what they desired was almost impossible. "You can make it if you really work hard, but, you see, sometimes hard work and strong determination aren't enough. You've got to think of how to survive here first, and then think about how to make enough money to afford your trip. Your departure date and time depend on how fast you make your travel money. Then again, you'll also need to think about how and where to save the money. You can't use the bank. You have to carry your money with you wherever you go like a mobile ATM. I'm sure you don't need me to spell out what that means."

"What? Travel money? Save money? Carry money? What money? Where? How?" Joy never asked one question at a time.

"Calm down, Joy. You're asking too many questions, and the wrong ones at that." Charity intervened to save the situation. "How do we raise the money? Is it possible to get a well-paying job that will pay off in no time? We're ready to do anything, I mean anything."

Faith knew this was the time to take them through their job description. "Look, if you think you'll find a job here, then you might as well wait for the rest of your lives. There are no jobs here or anywhere else. You create the job you want, you do it, and you decide how much you want to be paid."

"Sounds exciting. Can you explain this a little further?" Charity took control of the situation and spoke on behalf of the others.

"Call it general merchandise. The first golden rule is to use what you've to get what you want. Your greatest assets and money bags are right there in front of you. If you really want to make it snappy, then you'll want to consider expanding your business horizon to include …"

"Include what? What else should we expect now? Drink our own blood?" Joy was always the one who vocalised her doubts and emotions without warning.

"Calm down! It's not like I'm asking you to kill here. Call it making money from those who aren't smart enough to know how to keep their hard-earned money and valuables safe. If you want to look at it differently, it's like helping them to spend their money wisely, say for humanitarian purposes."

"So we'll become thieves as well as being prostitutes. What else? How bad can this get?" Joy was gripped with fear of the unknown.

"You can be couriers of drugs and firearms. This is the real thing, the big time. Girls, just one deal and you're instantly in Europe, no questions asked. There is one more last route though, a mind-blowing one, but let me warn you straightaway that it's definitely not for the cowardly. It's for those who are able to take the bull by the horns without apology."

Joy thought she had heard it all. In a moment she would be metamorphosed into a complete stranger. She would sell her body for money. She would steal from people, cheat, tell lies, peddle drugs, and traffic arms to be used in genocidal and fratricidal wars. For a moment she thought it was time to make a cost-benefit analysis. Was it really worth all the trouble? Was Europe really worth all the sacrifice? She was in a dilemma. She could not return home. She did not want to consider the option of remaining in Tripoli like Faith. She did not have her guts, her shrewd awareness, her seasoned experience, or the resourcefulness necessary to survive in this difficult, dangerous, and unfriendly environment. Joy felt that she lacked only one ingredient Faith had. Joy had faith in God. For Faith, everything was determined by fate and casualness. She was not conditioned by a value or belief system that questioned her choices. She did not believe in the existence of a world other than this one. She could not fathom the possibility of the remote scene of the final judgement, where she would be called to give account. If she had any account at all to give, it was not of herself but only of those who had made her the person she had become, starting with the criminal who took her innocence by force at the age of fourteen.

As for Joy, it was the time for reckoning. The only invariable factor was her unshakable faith which needed to be unshackled. The problem remained when and how. She was absolutely clueless. She had to hold on to something in order to believe there was an alternative to her selling her soul to the devil in exchange for the journey to a destination both unknown and uncertain.

"Joy, I know you're a woman of God. I know what's on your mind. You think all these things are wrong, but you didn't bring yourself here, so it's not your fault. God will understand whatever you do to survive and escape this situation." Faith knew her business sufficiently well to know both the right chord to touch and when to strike. Her instincts had never failed her in the past. "You know what, Joy? The last option I had in mind could be suitable for you. You do not need to sleep with anyone or do anything you consider wrong. My only reservation is whether or not you'll be able to pull it off."

Joy could not believe what she had just heard. A sinless option! Her faith would prevail after all, but only after she had carefully listened to what was involved.

"You can sell one of your kidneys. Everyone has got two, so you can comfortably sell one and still live a regular healthy life with just one. Look at me. There's nothing I've not been through. I've done everything humanly possible to survive in this place. I've done all the things I suggested you could do to make money. I didn't read them from a book. I learnt them from life, the greatest teacher. I've committed more abortions than I can possibly remember. When I didn't freely trade my body, men took me by force for free. I've been in and out of jail. Life in prison is not much different from life elsewhere. I've been involved in different kinds of crime, hoping to be picked up by the police, but they've completely given up on me as a nuisance. They know I'm untouchable. They wouldn't want people to hear what I've got to say about them. They're all corrupt greedy criminals and rapists, all of them from top to bottom. Would you believe me if I told you that I've sold one of my kidneys? Do I look like someone who's living with just one kidney? Unbelievable but true! If I could live with no kidneys at all, I'd have no problems. I'd sell the only one I still have and make some really good cash like I did before—more than the first time now that I know the market value of a healthy kidney."

"What do you mean by the market value of a human kidney? How much are we looking at here?" Charity interrupted anxiously. She was the queen of dreams. The thought of large sums of money tickled her more than anything else in the world.

"I got 50,000 euros. That was five years ago. It should've gone up much higher than that by now, even by fifty per cent."

"So you mean to tell us that you got that much money and you're still here! What did you do with it? Why didn't you proceed to Europe instead of remaining permanently in transit?" Charity could not believe her.

"I was too young, restless, naïve, and inexperienced. I didn't know the worth of money then. If I'd known what I know now, things would definitely have been different. You never know how useless and valueless money can be until you run into an entire room full of it. The first thing you think of when you come across so much money is that you'll never be in need of it again. It gives you false hope, security, and comfort. You'd never in your wildest dream imagine that it could end, just like that, as if it had vanished into thin air, as if you'd never had so much of it, as if you'd never had any of it. In my own case, I can't even give account of how 50,000 euros came into the palm of my hand and left at the same speed with which it came. My parents were anxious about me sending them money from Europe. My auntie who brought me to this place had promised them huge sums of money. My father was counting on it to build himself the house of his dream, marry another wife, and bribe his way through obtaining a chieftaincy title to give him recognition and visibility among his peers in the village. I couldn't let him down. That was why I had to sell my kidney. It was not for me to travel abroad. After all, why was I going to Europe if not to fulfil my father's dreams which I've already fulfilled here? They don't even know that I'm still in Africa, lost in transit. All they care about is the huge sums of money they receive from the daughter they are so proud of, the one who's succeeding where even men like my own father failed. I've not returned home now for five years, I might never see *Naija* again. My life's here now. I can't go back and bring shame on the same people I made so proud of having a daughter rather than a son. This is the ultimate price I've had to pay, and I'm doing my best."

"So the thought of living a different and possibly better life never ran through your mind? Not even once? Are you not tired of living in this dangerous place? If I were you, I'd want to set my feet at least once in Europe to see how it looks." Charity was trying to provoke Faith further.

"It's as if I was never really meant to see Europe. I should've been there to undergo the surgery when one of my kidneys was exported. It could've been done somewhere in Italy, but the associated risks were too many. First there was the problem of immigration and border control. Then again, my age. Then if things had gone wrong, I would have risked remaining permanently in a hospital bed or as a street prostitute for the rest of my life. But the main reason why I didn't travel had to do with my Madame. If I'd travelled to Italy, she would have traced me and forced me to sleep with her exclusive client who requested a virgin, and then she would have made away with all the money. There was no guarantee that she would have fulfilled all the promises she made to my father. At least this way I've been able to keep all the money for myself without having to pay her. Here I'm my own boss. I have my freedom, my connections, and my protectors. It's a horrifying place, but I've learnt the rules of the game of survival. I'm a survivor. I think I'm just fine here. I know I'm as good as dead, but at least I'm alive."

The girls were petrified at the end of Faith's story. It was emotionally draining and disheartening. There was dead silence. Each girl retired into her thoughts to carefully digest the muddle and terror that had just came down so heavily on them like a stormy wave. They were all faced with the most difficult decision. They were not in the right frame of mind to engage in anything rational. They knew in the deepest and most silent corner of their hearts that they had no alternative than to move on, come what may. Their greatest challenge now was how to raise the money. For this too they had individually decided how to go about it. It was only a question of time. The long-desired Europe was only a hundred kilometres away or a little more. They could almost see the Italian coast at the other end of the spectrum of the Mediterranean at sunset. It was too late to go back now.

# Chapter Eight

Three months later the girls were ready to make their journey to Europe at long last. While Hope and Charity got themselves involved in various dubious deals to raise the required money, Joy had spent most of the time convalescing from kidney surgery. She was only offered 10,000 euros for a healthy sound young kidney, as good as new. Faith had taken twenty per cent of the total sum as the deal mediator. Joy had barely enough to pay for her transfer, but that was all that mattered as long she did not have to sleep with men or do anything contrary to her over-sensitive conscience.

The Libyan coast of Misrata was a carnival of desperately impoverished people. There were promising young men of college or university age and women, mostly pregnant women with children of all ages. The coast was an agglomerate of people from Eritrea, Somalia, and Mali, along with people from Ghana, Niger, and Nigeria. Almost all the pregnant women had very young children of breast-feeding age, which they tied to their backs with pieces of cloth that looked like they would easily give way at the slightest brusque movement. All of them seemed to be in a scorching hurry to go somewhere and nowhere in particular. Their ill-concealed faces betrayed their desire to lose sight of the coast in order to face the perilous crossing of the immense ocean before them to their dream destination country in Europe. There was an overpowering aura of haste, as people tried to escape from the past for various reasons. Some were running away from wars and the consequent persecution, others from poverty and joblessness. Whatever reasons they had for their individual plight and their courage to dare the troubled waters of the deep Mediterranean Sea, they all seemed to nurture the unrelenting and profound hope in a better future for themselves and their families. They had paid exorbitant amounts of money to Libyan, Tunisian, Somali, and Sudanese traffickers. Some had sold their entire life belongings, mortgaged lands and properties, and forced their young daughters into arranged and premature marriages in order to embark on this one-way journey of hope. Men who were unable to pay were severely tortured, beaten, and threatened. Women were gang-raped and their young daughters' virginity mercilessly taken away.

Joy, Charity, and Hope grew suspicious at the sight of the several hundreds of people who had turned up at the coast at twilight to start the journey that was estimated to last only a couple of hours. It was when the fishing boat that was to convey the crowd appeared at the edge of the sea that they knew that what they had been through before was child's play. Their battleground gradually shifted under their feet. It moved from solid dry land to the waters. They came face to face with death, and they felt it right to their bone marrow.

"Come on! There are many people who are dying to take your place if you've changed your mind and don't want to travel anymore." The boat assistant screeched as he helped them to get on board. They scuffled and pushed their way through, not caring about the other passengers on the same adventure. "First the children! Let the children come in first and the pregnant mothers." He continued to scream at the top of his voice, improvising the much-needed microphone. They listened with deaf ears. Everyone tried to push his or her way through with the tenaciousness of people escaping from a sinking *Titanic*.

An hour later three hundred despairing passengers had boarded the overcrowded fishing boat. They sailed away in great confusion amidst cries of joy and fear, with an all-empowering echo of hope in the bright future that lay only a few hours away. Joy settled in a small dark corner of the boat, buried in her thoughts as her ordeal of the last nine months flashed through her mind. She had spent so much time in transit that the final destination was no longer as appealing as it had been when the journey started. All she could see and feel was death, despair, anguish, and fear, like one who was being led blindfolded to a firing squad. She tried to pray but the words were not forthcoming. Fear's grip overpowered the strength of her faith. "It's time to go home," she said to herself, giving up all hope for survival.

Suddenly, the fishing boat started to develop problems with the engine, as if Joy's prayers had been heard and answered by the wrong god whose number had been dialled in error. The passengers felt the sound of the engine change as if it had been switched off purposely or had died a natural death. They panicked, shouted, cursed, wept, and even called on God or Allah to save them from a danger that was more than imminent and could not easily be avoided. The inconsolable cries of the children made the already bad situation worse as their helpless mothers threw themselves into tantrums.

"Calm down, everyone! The situation is under control." The Captain failed to reassure the passengers. His voice betrayed him. He knew that the situation was beyond control, that there was an emergency they were not even prepared for. The hooting cries of the women and children did not help matters.

"So this is it then? All the troubles to get out of misery, and all I get is an anonymous death in the middle of nowhere! Do something! Let somebody do something, anything!" A middle-aged passenger was shouting in terror. His appeal was acknowledged. Another passenger, who had been suffering a panic attack, lit a blanket to call attention to the distressed boat. The smoke started to spread rapidly. Passengers coughed like people suffering from chronic asthma. The fire grew and kindled the engine's petrol. Before they knew it, there was open fire. Instinctively, passengers began to hurl themselves into the sea. There was no time to negotiate whether to die by burning or drowning.

The Italian coastguard on patrol between the island of Lampedusa and Malta came to the rescue and to recover bodies, dead and alive. The Red Cross and other volunteer organisations were alerted, and all tried to help as much as they could. Fishermen on routine business were recruited to the recue team.

"You come out to fish, and all you catch are the dead bodies of Africans. Why do they keep coming here? Don't they read the papers? Only last week a similar boat capsized. I recovered ten bodies of women and three children. *Che tragedia!* Why are they turning our country into a cemetery? Very soon we won't even have a place to bury them anymore." The fisherman complained as he struggled to save the lives of those who had temporarily lost consciousness.

Hope was recovered but was lifeless. She had drunk petrol mixed with water before she drowned after throwing herself into the sea. She did not know how to swim. Her body was soaked in oil when she was found. Charity and Joy were taken to different migrant centres for first aid. Joy was taken to the Lampedusa temporary centre, together with other migrants, for questioning and assessment to ascertain if they qualified for political asylum.

Before Joy even had the chance to be assessed and questioned, two Nigerian men in their mid-thirties approached her. They introduced themselves as Favour and Viktor. They had been stationed in the island of Lampedusa for four months to monitor her arrival. They had been sent by Comfort to intercept her as soon as the boat arrived. Both men were as unfriendly and callous as most of the men who had accompanied her on the different stages of her journey. They also spoke very little, except when strictly necessary, exactly like Musa and the Colonel. They had come in a Fiat Cinquecento car. Viktor ushered Joy to the backseat and simply said, "We're going to Torino."

Joy had no idea whether he was referring to a person, place, or thing. She was very exhausted after the trip that almost claimed her young life, but she was happy to be alive at least. She did not bother to ask for food or drink.

They had become rare commodities in her routine. She was unaware of the sleep her body so needed until she crashed helplessly into a profound and painkilling slumber. By the time she woke up, Favour was just pulling out of *via di porta portese* into the adjacent street, leading to the block of flats where Mercy was waiting for them.

"Finally! Welcome to *Italo*. Make yourself comfortable. I'm Mercy, and your auntie Comfort has instructed me to take care of you. Don't worry, everything will be fine. People don't know what it means to travel to Europe until they experience it for themselves. Now you have your own story to tell, but never mind, all that's in the past now. You've finally made it, and that's all that really matters".

"Yes, Auntie."

"Just call me Mercy. This is *Italo*, not *Naija*, no need for long titles, you see? You've already started enjoying the benefits of living in a free and civilised land. Indeed, here everyone is equal. Do you know you can even choose to call your mother by name and no one will crucify you? Lest I forget, you must be very hungry. Let me welcome you with the original *Italo* delicacy. It's *spaghetti alla Bolognese*. You'll like it. You see? You've not even been in this country for an hour, yet you're about to enjoy its goodies. Here there's nothing like hunger. There is so much to eat that people actually avoid eating so as not to put on weight. Have you ever thought of the possibility of a place in this world where people refuse food when there are people dying of hunger back home?"

Joy could not be bothered about Mercy's monologue about freedom and abundance of food. These were not her priorities. Only one thing was on her mind, and the time to discuss it was now. "Auntie Mercy, …" She tried to initiate a conversation about what bothered her the most.

"Lesson number three. I've just told you not to call me auntie. You must learn to follow instructions and do exactly what you're told, otherwise you'll not survive in this environment. This isn't *Naija*."

"Sorry, Mercy. I wanted to find out about the job. When can I start?"

"You just arrived a couple of hours ago. Give yourself some time to rest properly. That'll be a topic for tomorrow. Good night."

Mercy retired into the only bedroom in the flat, leaving Joy alone to figure out that she had to sleep on the sofa bed they had been sitting on. As early as six o'clock the next morning, Mercy woke Joy up from her uneasy sleep. She had business to attend to in the outskirts of Torino.

Mercy had been one of Comfort's girls who had fully paid her dues. She had worked on the streets of Torino for four years to pay off the debt of 70,000 euros. With her debt paid, she felt it was her turn to upgrade herself to the business of recruiting girls to work for her, exactly as she had worked for Comfort. She knew the business in and out and had learnt every detail about it in her own skin and at her own expenses. She had handled newly arrived and intimidated girls like Joy. She knew her very first conversation with Joy was going to be the most important. She had planned this meeting to the smallest detail.

"I hope you had a peaceful sleep. Now it's time for business, it's time to talk about the job you came here for."

Joy was overwhelmed with enthusiasm. After all, her dream was going to come true. She could not but continue to thank goodness in her heart, but she remembered her good manners, which she was almost throwing to the winds out of excitement. "Auntie, I mean Mercy, I really thank you and Auntie Comfort for this trip. I'll never forget you. My God will bless and prosper you."

Mercy knew it was not the time to beat around the bush in a quagmire of explanations. She had to go straight to the point without getting caught up in logical details. "Before we talk about the job, we need to talk about your debt first."

. "Debt? Owing who? How? When? How much?"

"Let me break this down for you. Your auntie spent a lot of money to sponsor you to come over here. She paid for your transport, passport, and visa and even paid people at immigration to allow you to go through without much questioning. She also paid all those men who took care of you in transit, including Favour and Viktor, who spent four whole months waiting for you. If they hadn't come for you when they did, you'd have been deported back to Libya. Let me tell you, those they allow to stay here or go to other parts of Europe like Germany, Switzerland, France, or Spain are those they consider as fleeing from situations of wars and political or religious persecution. Your case is different. They'd have discovered this immediately you told them you're from Nigeria, and they'd have classified you as an economic migrant who isn't qualified for consideration. They're considered as illegal immigrants who break the law in order to come into the country. You're only allowed to come in illegally if you're running away from war, but not from poverty and unemployment. Do you remember Faith? She works for Comfort as well and has been generously paid for her services. I know she pretended not to know you, but this is one of the rules of the business: people work under cover. I'm aware she took twenty per cent of the money you earned, but that's her own way of making some extra cash for herself. Now all these things and people cost money. You're expected to pay them back before you can start earning your own money. In a nutshell, you owe your auntie Comfort the sum of 80,000 euros."

"You mean 80,000 naira?"

"Don't worry about the naira equivalent for now. We'll keep deducting it from your earnings until you've paid off everything. We won't cheat you on this, trust me."

"It's no problem as long as I get a job to do. Now, tell me, what's the job about? I'm really good at hairdressing, but I don't mind doing anything else like baby-sitting, cleaning, working in a shop, or even in a restaurant."

"Now you must listen to this. Have you seen a hairdresser or cleaner build a house in your entire life? What makes you think that hairdressing here pays more than it does in *Naija*? Do you think that hair is made of gold here? Have you travelled all the way to Europe just to work as a hairdresser? Have you forgotten that you even did hair free of charge in the village? What makes you think it would fetch so much money in so little time?"

"Hmm, that makes sense though. But if I can't do any of these jobs, what else can I do? I didn't go to school. I can't work in an office."

"The secret is having a product or a service that's not available here, one that sells like hot cakes. Don't you remember the times your auntie brought in jewellery from Dubai and how women queued up to buy it? Does that mean there's no jewellery in *Naija*? No, it means people just want exclusive things from a different country. The same thing applies to our business here in *Italo* that I'm about to expose you to. You see, all *Italo* men like the silky and dusky skin of black girls. They like their curvy shapes like the full-blown moon. They prefer our girls with some meat to their bones, unlike their wives who are perpetually on diets. They like the way our girls take care of them like Mama Africa."

"Am I going to look after men?"

"No, they're going to look after you if you do your job well. Some of them will come to you for a first-hand experience, some will come to you for fun, some for pure adventure, and others because they can ask you what they dare not even think of asking their diet-addicted wives. Look, if you're lucky they could make you their mistress or assistant wife. They'll take you shopping, take you on holidays, pay for your flat and all your bills, and even marry you just to help you to get the red passport and licence to remain in Europe for ever!"

"I still don't get it. Am I to get married to an *Italo* man?"

"I'm not asking you to do anything different than you did in Libya. I'm not even asking you to do anything different from what all women do. The only difference is that you could be making loads of money if you're smart enough to sell to your market. In the simplest terms, you have to sleep with men, short and simple."

Joy did not understand Mercy's last words. She thought she did not hear her right. She maintained her calm and allowed Mercy all the time she needed to explain what she was sure she did not hear.

"It's not a big deal. Things have changed. This is the 21st century. Call it import and export or simply the business of demand and supply. Europeans used to come to Africa to exchange what they had for what they needed from Africa. Today, it's the other way round. We bring what we have into Europe and exchange it for raw cash. The world has become a global market. Everything is for sale as long as there's a ready market for it. Our kind of business thrives mainly here in *Italo* because of the unruliness of their men and their unlimited demand for paid sex."

Sex! Paid sex! That was the hint Joy was looking for. She could no longer pretend not to have heard. The cards were on the table open before her, and there was no more room for pretence. "So that's it! My auntie brought me here to do prostitution, to be a prostitute!"

"Not exactly. It depends on the professional angle you want to place on your business. These days, everything is about professionalism and presentation. Just for the record, nobody is a prostitute. The word now is escort, operating at different levels. At the highest level you could be an escort to important people like presidents, politicians, footballers, and celebrities. The sky is your limit!"

Joy's greatest nightmare had just become a reality. Was this what her life had been preserved for? Was this what it meant to fulfil her purpose as a woman of destiny? She would have preferred to be drowned a million times over than to be a sex worker. She had even sold one of her kidneys to avoid being tarnished. Now there was no escape, not in this foreign land. She did not even know where she was. She could not call for help if she wanted to. The only familiar face was the face of the one person who was going to lead her directly through the gates of hell. This was the answer to her prayers, her dream come true that would improve her prospects in life and wipe out the curse of poverty from the face of her family forever—but at the cost of her own soul. She did not know what to think of or worry about any more. Was it the promising life of a pastor's wife that she left unfulfilled or was it her education that now had no further hope of resuscitation? Was it the debt she had incurred even without knowing or the fear of the unknown risks and hazards of working on the streets of a country that was contradiction personified? Whatever the case, she knew there was no going back. It was too late to do so now.

"So when do I start?"

"Good question! The right question! Now you must listen to me carefully, I need to explain a few things to you, but first let me be clear with you. The 80,000 euros you owe your auntie doesn't include your upkeep. You'll have to pay for your food, clothes, transportation, rent and *joint*. There's also a common purse to which you must contribute weekly. It's used for emergencies such as tips for the boys and police who give us important information."

All of this sounded so unfamiliar to her. She was curious only about one word. "*Joint*? What's that?"

"It's your place of work, the ground on which you stand to wait for clients. You'll have to pay for it, otherwise others won't allow you to operate there. Don't worry too much about that. You don't need to go too often to your joint. There have been some major changes, and it's now too dangerous to work permanently on the streets, I've made all the arrangements. You'll live in a flat, and your clients will come in there to see you, Favour will be the one in charge of your flat. Make sure you collaborate with him, as you'll not like what you'll see if you get him angry. I'm afraid there's too much to take in, but don't worry, you'll get to learn with time. Just relax for now. There's no time to waste. You leave tomorrow with the 7.30 train for Rome."

# Chapter Nine

In the early hours of the following day, Mercy accompanied Joy to the *porta nuova* central train station in Torino to board a *frecciarossa* high speed train to *stazione termini* in Rome. She had been instructed about all she needed to know in order to travel safely alone without drawing any attention to herself. The journey was to last approximately four hours with a few stops at major stations.

When the train finally pulled up at its final stop in Rome, Joy remained in the tenth coach as she had been told, waiting for Favour to meet her right on the train. They made their way towards the bus station to board the bus route 105 towards *via casilina*. They jumped into the overcrowded bus that was ready to move without any warning to its passengers and squeezed themselves in a corner. They did not bother to buy a valid ticket. Favour was very familiar with this route. It was mainly used by migrants, especially Africans. He knew no ticket inspector would be courageous enough to show up, and he would not find the space even if he wanted to. If he did find a space by some miracle, he knew it would be a wasted effort.

Most of the passengers were clandestine without jobs or any means of livelihood. They could not afford to feed themselves, let alone pay for a ticket. They carried large polythene carrier bags full of their sub-standard wares, such as socks, handkerchiefs, singlets, T-shirts, pillowcases, bed sheets and table cloths. These mobile marketers of mainly Nigerian origin had gradually replaced the majority of Senegalese *"vous compra"*, as they were popularly called. Their Nigerian comrades were known as *"signora buon giorno"*. They spent all day hawking their products from one building to the other and from door to door. They were often seen as a nuisance. Housewives had to open the doors of their homes, only to come face to face with a hungry black man trying to make a living by encroaching on their priceless privacy. Some of these women simply insulted them, others unpleasantly invited them to return to their country of origin, and others simply slammed the door in their face. The more sensitive ones gave them money without even looking at the items that they considered completely out of place in their elegant and ridiculously well-kept homes. "*Grazie signora!*" they would say, excited at making some extra cash with their goods still intact, becoming beggars in the process.

Joy felt relieved when they alighted from the bus after an hour or so amidst the heavy Roman traffic, typical of the busiest time of the day. She was long-suffering. The packed bus reminded her of the ill-fated boat from the coast of Libya to the island of Lampedusa. They made their way along a semi-deserted and unpaved road to a large dilapidated building that looked like a wrecked and abandoned warship.

"This is the place" were Favour's only words as he disappeared to attend to other pressing businesses. Joy found herself in an inhospitable room in a two-bedroom apartment. She could see other buildings in the vicinity, but her apartment was rather secluded from the others as if it was not originally included in the town-planning scheme. It was as lifeless as it was isolated. The sitting area had only a three-seat sofa and a fourteen-inch television. The kitchen was a complete empty space, with no sign of cooking supplies or food. The gas cooker was unconnected to any gas cylinder or supply of electricity. The only functional gadget in the entire kitchen was a made-in-China microwave. Joy's room had only a single mattress on the floor and a light bulb over her head, hanging from the ceiling like the sword of Damocles. All she could do here was lie down or sleep.

No person, animal, or thing, except the four thick pallid walls and her thoughts, kept her company. Three days had passed since she last saw Favour. There was no sign of him or any other person in the flat. She occasionally sneaked out to the kitchen to drink some water but hurried back to her room. She was terrified at the thought of being found outside the boundaries of her own territory. She had been in Italy now for almost a week, but there was nothing to remind her that she was indeed in the so-much-desired land of promises. She felt worse than she had felt in transit. Then at least she was always in the company of Hope and Charity. With them she could vocalise her fears and share common aspirations. Now she was all alone. Her thoughts for a moment drifted to Charity. What could have happened to her now? Was she not one of Comfort's girls too? Why were they not together now? Charity's presence would have made a whole world of difference. She was the one person who knew how to find reasons to smile through tears in every situation.

She was still deeply absorbed in her thoughts when she suddenly heard some strange movements. It was someone trying to enter the apartment with a jangling bunch of keys like a janitor. She hurriedly tip-toed back to her room, switched off the light, and lay down quietly on the mattress. She heard heavy steps pacing up and down the tiny apartment, as one ensuring that everything was in order. Then there was dead silence. Just when she began to regain her calm, thinking the intruder was gone, she felt a heavy figure descend on her unexpectedly like a predator. He was too strong for her, weakened as she was by prolonged hunger. He overpowered her effortlessly, tore her clothes, and forcefully had his way with her in the dark room as she struggled to wrestle with a shadow. Her cries for help could not be heard by anyone. No one was meant to hear her. When he had had his fill, he disappeared almost exactly as he had stolen in, like a thief in the middle of the night.

Joy had just lost what she held most precious and sacred. She had often fantasised about her first wedding night. She had vowed never to give herself to anyone except the man who was to be her lawfully wedded husband. She had even opted to lose a kidney in order to preserve her innocence and uprightness. Now she had just lost it in the middle of nowhere to a complete stranger without a name or identity. She remained miserably immobile for the next two days. She had no more tears as her fountain of tears seemed to have dried up all of a sudden. Her voice was beginning to sound hoarse, toneless, wobbly, and strangulated. She had lost the will to live. She was left with nothing else to live or die for.

She gathered her last strap of strength to creep out of the room when the feeling of hunger got the better of her. Miraculously, she stumbled on some pizza with pepperoni, mozzarella, and gorgonzola cheese. The stranger had left it on his historic visit. She was too hungry to ask questions. She devoured the pizza with the hunger and anger of someone returning from a hunger strike. The last meal she remembered was the *spaghetti alla Bolognese*, her meal of welcome offered by Mercy.

The keys to the apartment turned again. It was Favour. He came in carrying shopping bags containing food and clothing items, including some toiletries, which he discarded in the bathroom area. "Get ready. Take a shower, change your clothes, look nice, and smell fresh. Your first appointment in is two hours' time." Favour tried to sort out the shopping bags as he gave his orders.

Appointment? In two hours' time? She had no clue what he was talking about. She did not even have any concept of the time. She could only distinguish night from day by the rising and setting of the sun. What could he possibly mean? Was she going out to meet someone or was someone coming in to see her? She remembered Mercy's warnings about infuriating Favour. The little she already knew about him pointed to the fact that he never liked being asked silly questions. He took it for granted that the few words he muttered were more than enough for any rational being to make sense of. At least she did understand that she had to prepare herself, and that was already a good starting point. The doorbell rang exactly two hours later. A scruffy looking man in his early sixties came in.

"This is your first appointment for today. He's here to sample you. If you behave properly and he likes you, then he'll move from being a customer to becoming a client. He's just coming back from work as you can see. He runs his own business as a bricklayer. He has all his earnings for the day in his pocket. I know his type. If he really likes you, he'll come here every day on his way from work, and guess what? He'll deposit all his money with you as if with a bank. Men like him have nothing else to live for except some exciting encounter, which I'm sure you're ready to give him."

Joy did not need any further explanation. It was her first job, the first of many others to come. She had nothing else to lose.

"That wasn't a bad start at all," Favour said as he flaunted some euro notes left by her first customer. She had no idea how much she had earned. "You'll have no problems at all with me if you carry on this way. Come on! It's time to celebrate the success of your first job. Let's have some fun. He did not wait for an answer. He grabbed her in surprise and pushed her back into the small room and onto the mattress on the floor. He ravaged her with the strength and stench of the intruder who stole her virginity in the shadows of darkness. Joy had no more doubts. Favour was that familiar stranger. He left her almost lifeless and made his way out of the door, humming some tune of victory. His day had paid off both in cash and in kind. He headed for a nearby money shop to wire some of his profits to his promised spouse in Benin City.

Joy remained submerged in her thoughts about what had just happened. She could not make a rational connection between the intruder and Favour. Why did he behave that way when he could have openly declared his intentions without hiding behind an aura of mystery? Did he intentionally do that to frighten her? What else could she possibly expect from a man who was revealing himself to have more than a dozen shades of grey? He had raped her on two different occasions with two different identities. She passed out at the thought that these episodes were going to be part of her routine. She was gradually being tutored to become an automated sex machine.

Over the weeks that followed, the bricklayer's visits became an everyday occurrence as Favour had anticipated. He came, sometimes in Favour's absence, did his business, and left the pre-negotiated amount of money on a designated small table in one corner of the sitting room. *Arriverderci* was the only word he used. Joy had no idea what this meant and could not care less. For her it signified that his business for the day was over and he was on his way out. Favour's rape had become as constant as the routine of the bricklayer's visit. Joy felt herself violated time and time again by both men. There was no significant difference between who paid for her services and who did not. All she was required to do was to be receptive when the occasion demanded.

Favour returned in the early hours of one morning and woke Joy up from her restless sleep. "We must discuss. Things have changed, and you must be ready for your next assignment."

Joy had learnt how to read his mind. He had first used the word "appointment" when the bricklayer came to the flat on visits. Now she was learning fast enough to understand that an "assignment" would definitely mean something quite different from the home stopovers.

"You'll leave for *Viterbo* tomorrow with the seven o'clock train from the *stazione termini*," he said. "It is about an hour's journey. You'll need to stop at the *porta fiorentina* station and wait for further instructions. I've arranged everything, so you need not worry. Just obey instructions. Look, here is all you need." He handed her a plastic bag full of skinny jeans, trousers and miniskirts, see-through tops, high-heeled shoes, make-up, wigs, condoms, and contraceptive pills. She had no idea about the contents of the bag. Her mind flashed back to Musa in Niamey, Niger who had handed them a similar plastic bag of *hijab* and *chador*. Those clothes concealed them from head to toe. They veiled every trace of femininity. These clothes were the exact opposite. They were intended to uncover what was meant to be covered. Joy had to figure out for herself that the word "*Viterbo*" must be the name of a place or city. She remembered Mercy telling her of a train to Rome. Taking a train had come to mean some form of movement from one city to another.

Joy stopped at the *porta fiorentina* station in *Viterbo* as she had been told. She stood still on the platform at which the trained had arrived. She was immediately approached by a medium-sized man who needed no introduction. It was Viktor, the same man who, together with Favour, had abducted her from the questioning session in the migrant reception centre in the island of Lampedusa.

"Follow me! I've got the car parked a few metres away from the train station. I'm taking you to where you'll work tonight."

The word "*joint*" suddenly flashed through her mind. She remembered what Mercy said about what that place meant—the actual ground or spot where she was expected to stand while waiting to be perused like a newly launched website and be picked up by potential clients. How could she have forgotten? Mercy had highlighted that it had to be paid for as well. Everything about Europe was about money owed. No one seemed to be talking about money earned. Who else would she owe apart from Comfort, Mercy, Favour, Viktor and now the sole administrator of a misappropriated public ground? She tried with little or no success to forget about her ordeal. She tried to focus on the task she was about to undertake—her very first night as a street sex worker.

"Here you are." Viktor finally pulled up in a dark corner of the road in the outskirts of the ancient Tuscan city of the Lazio region. He drove away without further instructions, leaving her to figure things out for herself. For a moment, she thought her world had ended. She felt as though she had been abandoned to herself to die in the cool summer evening breeze of early September, which felt to her as strong and harsh as the bleak and biting winter cold. Everything around her was silence. It was dark and isolated and there was no sign of any living being within a radius of ten miles. She could not help but think of the four unfriendly walls that protected her and how unsafe, lonely, and threatened she now felt. Compared to where she found herself now, she would have preferred to be at the mercy of the unannounced and ravaging visits of the bricklayer and Favour a thousand times.

A car similar to Viktor's *Fiat cinquecento* suddenly stopped, and three girls got out as the car drove away hurriedly. Joy felt relieved. She finally had company. The girls were dressed in unimaginable outfits that reminded her only of the biblical story of Sodom and Gomorrah. They wore high-heeled shoes that looked and felt like an invitation to madness and suicide. They laughed and giggled like lottery winners. Joy could not understand how girls in her same condition could be so happy and enchanting. They must have a secret, and she was determined to find out.

"*Ashawo!*" one of the girls called out. "We have a *jambite*. What's your name? What do you prefer to call yourself?"

Joy took a breath as she tried to understand the difference between what her name was and what she would like to call herself, wondering if there really was any difference.

"Miss No Name, yes, that's your new name until you make up your mind to answer."

"Leave her alone! Her name's Joy. She's Victor's new girl, the one he told us about, remember?"

Gift sounded friendly and welcoming. She reminded Joy of Charity. Although Gift had been working on the streets for the past four years, she was uncontaminated by the greed and heartlessness imposed on her by the menacing demands of working in the hustle lane. "Come, my dear, don't mind them. Everything will be fine. We were once like you. I'll tell you all you need to know and how to survive in this dangerous environment."

Joy felt a stream of liberation. Gift was the kind of person she needed. She was a gift indeed by name, in words and action.

"First things first," Gift went on. "Before you know the rules of the job, you need to look like you're on the job. Do you have any appropriate working clothes?"

Joy remembered the polythene bag she was holding absent-mindedly. "Here."

They went through the contents of the bag, and Gift took her through the induction drill. "Go to that corner and wear these. Now listen. Here you have some condoms. We call them rubbers or raincoats, if you really want to last on this job and look forward to a normal life at the end of this valley of tears, you must make sure you use them. I mean ask your clients to use them. Don't get greedy over how much they offer to pay you. Some want to do it without, and they offer you more money, but if you love your life, you must protect yourself from the perils of this business."

"Madame Lecturer!" shouted one of the girls, who was nicknamed First Lady. "Teach her the proper way to make good money sharp! Sharp! Do you think everyone wants to die on this job like you? Why should I settle for a miserable twenty euros when the guy is able to cough out a hundred bucks? I'm not daft, you know. Let me tell you the secret. Forget about those white lies about AIDS and all that crap. It won't get to you if it's not your portion, but if it's your portion—your destiny, if you like—let him wear two at a time, it will still happen."

"Don't listen to her." Gift tried to pull Joy away from the distractions of First Lady. "Are you not a born-again Christian? I'm a Muslim, but I pay my tithes, both at home and abroad. I also have so many prayer warriors and pastors with powerful anointing praying for my protection that I'm fully fortified. The devil has deleted my number from his contact list", concluded First Lady. "Secondly, don't allow any of the clients to take you to an unknown place. For a start, I'd encourage you to do your business just behind here." Gift took her to the back of a bush and pointed at an old mattress. "Here you're safe and no one's going to harass you. If anyone tries to be violent, we'll be here to defend you."

"Have you told her that these guys pay more when they drive you away in their cars to the place of their choice, where they really feel more comfortable to demand the services they require?" First Lady always believed that people have choices and should have all possible options to choose from.

"Yes, where they feel comfortable indeed to rape you without paying, to kill and bury your body with no questions asked. Have you forgotten how many of our girls have disappeared just like that? It's better to be safe than sorry."

"That's true, I think I prefer to remain here for a start and enjoy your protection for now until I'm steadier."

"Wise decision," Gift concluded with satisfaction.

At the end of the working evening, which started with the arrival of the first clients towards eleven o'clock and concluded at four-thirty, Joy had attended to twenty clients. Her average fee was twenty euros. Some clients, who had learnt from the way the girls haggled and hiked up their prices, were unscrupulous and paid as little as five euros per encounter. Joy had a bag full of euros, mainly in denominations of tens and twenties, which the clients dropped at a corner of the thick bush. Viktor came quickly to accompany her back to the *porta fiorentina* train station, where she was to board the early morning train used by commuters who work in Rome. It was too early and ungodly an hour to attract the attention of ticket inspectors. Favour was anxiously waiting for her to return. He dragged the polythene bag off her and searched voraciously for the proceeds of the evening as Joy staggered her way towards the bedroom to make up for a memorable night. Wow! 300 euros!

This was Joy's routine for the next two weeks. She was picked up by Viktor and driven to the chosen *joint* for the night. Then he returned to pick her up again in the early hours of the next day and accompanied her to the train station where she boarded bus 105, headed for *casilina*. Joy still had no idea of how much money she had made, what she had paid off, and what was left of her debt. She had been away from home now for close to a year, most of which had been spent in transit. She had been working for three weeks now, seeing an average of twenty clients a day, not counting the home visits of the bricklayer which had become a daily affair.

She returned home one morning after working in the *magliana* area in the suburbs of Rome. It had been a terrific night. The girls, including First Lady, Gift, and Joy, had worked competitively, together with other girls from Albania, Moldavia, and Russia. There was an unanticipated police raid. Unlike other times, they had not been forewarned by their insider informant, *Maresciallo Sciagallo*.

"*Ogbalegbe*!" First Lady had alerted the other girls. She was always the alarmist whose instincts and perception of danger were far more developed than those of a cocaine-sniffing police dog. They descended on the girls like an explosion of the Etna volcano. They had to run for their lives, taking every possible route of escape. Joy found herself back home with the help of a potential client, who impulsively came to the help of this damsel in distress.

It was the one experience she needed to give her a wakeup call to wonder about how she had become the next-door neighbour to death itself. She had prayed to God to spare her life, with the resolve never to return to this death-defying way of life. She had challenged God to a duel in the pangs of an impromptu death. Now that her prayers had been answered, she knew there was no turning back. She felt she had been miraculously delivered, even without her knowing or wanting it.

# Chapter Ten

Joy got home safely and was reassured by Favour's absence. She had enough time to stage-manage her next point of action before he returned.

She ran the tap and filled the tub to the brim, emptying in all the shower gels and bath foams she could lay her hands on. She immersed herself in the water and allowed herself to be caressed by its energising and soothing aromatherapy. Her life in the past year came vividly alive in front of her as if she was watching a home video. She saw a young and vibrant girl full of dreams and aspirations for a better life for herself and her family. She saw how those dreams became ignited by the promise of a trip to Italy and allowed herself to re-live all the strong emotions she had felt when she took the first trip to Benin City, then the exciting trip to Lagos, and the once-in-a-lifetime experience of a flight from Lagos to Niamey in Niger. The show of her life stages now was taken over by the extremely unforeseen circumstances of her transit saga, climaxing in her unbelievable arrival in the island of Lampedusa, after coming too close for comfort to death and losing a journey companion and close acquaintance to the deep and mysterious waters of the Mediterranean.

Then her shattering affairs with life in the sex industry played back through her mind. She could not reconcile this dramatic movie with herself. What she saw was not a true reflection of her dreams and expectations. Where did it all go wrong? She asked herself.

Reality began to dawn on her as the water in the tub gradually became cold, reminding her that it was almost winter, that she was in Europe, and that the story in the movie she had just watched as a spectator was in fact her own story.

It was reckoning time. She estimated how many years she would have to work in order to extinguish her outstanding debt of 80,000 euros, besides her calculated costs of living. She carefully thought about how many men she would have to sleep with and how old she would be by the time she would be free to work for herself and make her own money. She began to grasp the madness behind this whole arrangement and wondered why she had not stopped to think about it until now.

She broke into a cry of liberation and started to scrub herself hysterically, as if she could wash away all that she had been through and become a new person with a brand new story to tell. She emerged from the bathtub a different person from the one who was submerged. She found her way to the under-used kitchen, made a sandwich, and opened a bottle of *Lambrusco* wine. It was time to celebrate the beginning of a long battle to come.

She heard a familiar noise coming from the front door of the apartment. Favour came in, using the same bunch of keys he had used the first night he had raped her. At last she had the evidence she had been looking for, apart from his body mass and odour, which she felt and smelt in the darkness of her room when he took her by force. Fresh and clean! He struggled to start a conversation with her for the very first time. He knew something had changed. He knew he was standing before a different person. The person he left would not dare to take a shower, let alone a bath, and open his *Lambrusco* without permission. He knew there was trouble. He needed all his acting skills to pull through.

"Come on, baby girl, it's been a while. I've really missed you. You know I like you a lot."

Joy could not believe the words she had just heard. He reminded him of the lying village boys who would tell her anything that came across their minds just to have her attention. Her mind swiftly went back to Pastor Joshua, the only man who had truly loved her without doing so much as taking her by the hand. She knew Favour was trying to mend fences, but she would not be so easily bought over by the shadows of a counterfeit romance.

"I know what you did. I know it was you."

"Me? What?"

"It was you who raped me on the first night I came. Why did you have to drive so much fear into me?"

It was pointless for him to show any sign of remorse. He was not the type. He hated being taken unawares. He did not see this coming, and he did not know what to say. He just stood there, thinking of his next point of action.

"Don't worry, it's all in the past now. I've forgiven you. I just want to let you know that you took away my virginity."

"You? A virgin? You should have told me!" He could not forgive himself for his business loss. He should have known. That would have been the real deal, the one good deal he needed to pull in order to make big money once and for all. He knew of clients who were ready to pay tens of thousands of euros just to have a virgin.

*The Sound of Silence*

"Anyway, it's game over. I'm done."

Her voice was so firm and decisive. He had never heard her speak this way before with an element of intimidation in her self-confidence.

"It's too early to quit. You've not even started growing in the business yet. Come on, give yourself some time. You'll get used to it, and before you know it, you'll be counting thousands of euros."

"I believed that once when I was under a spell. Now I know it's not really so. Surely there must be some 'normal' jobs in this country that I can do. I can't go to the streets anymore, and that's final."

"You don't even know what you're talking about. Have you ever heard of the recession? There are no jobs, not even for the *Italos* themselves. Businesses are folding up, and small scale businessmen are committing suicide every day. The youths are unemployed. Many of them are even leaving their own country for other countries in Europe like Germany and the United Kingdom. These are highly educated people with degrees in professional fields, yet they cannot find jobs in their own country. What chances have you got here? You don't even have the right documents to stay, you're not educated, you don't speak the language, and you're black."

"Black? What has my skin colour got to do with this?"

"It simply means that they'll never accept you as one of them, even if you marry an *Italo*, have an *Italo* passport, or live here for more than three decades. You'll always be a permanent foreigner, only good for cleaning their homes or their streets populated with their sex-hungry men."

"I came here to do an honest and decent job. I can work as a cleaner. All I know is that I'm not going back to the streets. It's too risky, and it's not what I came here for."

"Six euros an hour, that's your take-home as a cleaner."

"Some men offered five euros, some don't even pay at all, and some beat you up after using you. But that's not the main point. Mercy told me that I owe 80,000 euros which I have to pay back. I'd have to sleep with 4,000 men or twice each with 2,000 men. Even with an average of twenty encounters a day, it would take me ten years to earn that money as things stand now. By the time I paid off my debt, I'd be twenty-eight years old. When will I start earning my own money? Will I ever go back to school? Would you marry someone like me, even if I become stinking rich?"

Favour was unprepared for such hard talk. The girl had definitely done too much thinking. Favour hated women who were capable of using their own brains. They scared him and made him feel small and inadequate. He knew she was right, but only from her own point of view as the one being exploited. It was pure business and nothing more. He could not care less about who got hurt or how, who got used by whom or when. He should only see things from his own point of view and not that of his hallowed milk cow. Reasoning was not one of Favour's strengths, and he knew it. He could not by any means engage in an articulate argument, especially with a woman. It was time to strategise and move the ball to his comfort zone.

"We can make it work. Forget about paying back your auntie Comfort. What about having all the money to ourselves? I'm ready to marry you since I took your virginity. Trust me, I'm ready to accept my responsibility and make it up to you. What do you think?" He did not really expect her to say exactly what she thought about the situation at hand.

"On your life! Over my dead body, not after what you've done to me. I've forgiven you, but I can't bear the sight of a ruthless rapist like you."

"Did you just call me a rapist? I will pass on that because I really mean business. I've got no time to waste on frivolous women's talk about morality. I know you've got something up there in your brain, so let me tell you that you can't just walk away like that. You've obligations to fulfil, and this time I'm not referring to the money you owe your auntie, Mercy, and me." Joy wondered what his words meant. She was about to ask for further clarifications when he cut her short and continued his monologue. "You are under oath to pay back, otherwise …"

"Oath? When? Where? How?"

"Do you remember Barrister Bright?"

She could never have forgotten him. He was the traditional man of the gods who had made her to go into a small room in his chambers in Benin City. The more Joy tried to remember, the more confused she became. The only relevant detail she remembered was passing out. Everything else was blank.

"Yes."

Favour had seen the surprised expression on her face and knew that it was exactly the time to drop the bombshell. "He shaved off some of your pubic hairs when you were unconscious. They're now safely stored in his shrine. If you attempt to run away without repaying what you owe to the last euro cent, he'll use that as a point of contact to either harm you directly or to harm members of your family. If you decide not to pay your dues and remain in this country, you run the risk of going mad. You'll become a slave to yourself, you'll not be able to account for all the money you work for, you'll toil without results, you'll sow without reaping, and, worst of all, you'll become so visible to the police that they'll arrest you and deport you. I can see the look of your family members when you're deported on one of those charter flights from Milano Malpensa airport to Lagos. I can picture the scene with your picture on the front page of the dailies with the headline 'Nigeria's Shame'. I'm sure you never considered all these details in your little head."

Joy was completely without words. She was lost in thought.

"And I've not even told you about what they can do to your family back home."

"Okay! Stop! You don't need to be this cruel."

Favour knew that he had just won the jackpot. It was the end of the argument, at least for now. He imagined that she needed time to think over the new information that she had so unexpectedly received. He left and closed the door behind him without uttering a word. She had so much thinking to do, and she needed all the time in the world to do it.

He returned five days later and was rather pleased to find a more amenable Joy. He could read her mind like an open book. She had decided to stay—and possibly on his terms and conditions. It was mission accomplished for him. However, the music had just changed, and he had to make some modifications to its rhythm. He agreed to her refusal to work on the streets but insisted that she received more clients at home, apart from the bricklayer, whose patronage was never wanting.

Favour was not a skilled risk-taker. He did not want to risk losing the source of his golden eggs. Any freedom of movement away from the four walls of the apartment was an absolute taboo and a non-negotiable no-go area. In exchange, she could have her way as the woman of the house. She could cook, eat her favourite meals, and watch the television.

For the following months until Christmas, the television was Joy's only contact with the outside world. When she was not receiving clients, she spent her entire day watching all imaginable programmes on the national and private television stations, switching from one channel to the other. She particularly looked forward to daily romantic programmes such as *Mille vetrine*, *Un posto alla luna*, and the Italian version of the famous American soap *The Brave and the Beautiful*.

Although these programmes kept her busy and occupied her thoughts, she often thought about how difficult and complicated her situation had become. She needed more than a miracle in order to break free from her chainless bondage. She thought she had faith, but she realised that this was not enough in her circumstance. She could not believe beyond every reasonable doubt that indeed there was a way out of her predicament. The reality before her was concrete evidence that the answer was to be found far beyond faith. She had no alternative other than to abandon herself to time. Time heals all wounds, even if it leaves some scary scars. She consoled herself and waited patiently for the natural tides of time.

In the meantime, she had found an ally in the bricklayer, who finally revealed his name as Mimmo. She was surprised to discover that he knew some words in English and could make himself understood in the language.

He had worked with a road construction company for over fifteen years in different countries in West Africa, including Nigeria. He told Joy how he really enjoyed life in Africa, where people referred to him as "master" and where, as a white man, he was made to feel superior, a privilege that he never wanted to relinquish until he was catapulted back to Italy just when he had been hypnotized by everything on black soil. He returned to his home country as a misfit. He was near retirement. His two sons had been estranged from him, and his wife gave him the greatest surprise of his life when she invited him to go back where he came from. There was no longer room for him in her life and in their family home. He had to start a small business as a bricklayer just to keep him from the thoughts of taking his own life. He made a lot of money, and with that he sponsored his overindulgences in gambling and paid sex.

Joy could not believe him when he told her that he was made to leave a minimum payment of 200 euros each time he had paid her a visit. "We're both victims here," he said. "I had to pay more to protect my identity, since I don't want to expose my dirty patronage to the streets. It worked well for me. Again, I'm able to afford it, and I had nothing else to do with my earnings except to pay for some moments of pleasure."

There were some signs of regret in his voice now. He would never again have the courage to touch her, not after he had opened up to her. The dimensions of their relationship took a drastic turn, when Joy told him her own story. He could not forgive himself when he realised that she shared the same birthday with his second son. He felt like he had violated the daughter he never had. His entire life would never be long enough for him to make atonement. Joy was enthusiastic about the way things had changed between them. She saw this as a ray of light at the end of the dark tunnel. He continued to visit regularly and leave the same sum of money, but he never touched her again. Now he needed her more for her companionship than her services. They spent even longer periods of time together as time went by. He gave her money secretly and surprised her a great deal when at Christmas he offered to send the sum of 1,000 euros to her parents. This was the first time she had ever sent money home to them from Europe, and it was not money she made out of prostitution. She had reasons to hope that things would finally work in her favour at the appointed time. Favour could not be perturbed about the bond that was beginning to unfold between the two as long as his business interest was protected and the euros kept flowing in.

One morning Joy overheard a conversation between Favour and a strange woman, whom she later identified as Mercy from Torino. He was to go on another assignment to the island of Lampedusa. Joy intuited that others girls were due to arrive with the fishing boat from Libya and that Favour would need to be away for a week or more. This was the occasion she had been waiting for. She knew it was now or never.

Favour left two days later. Like other times, he did not specify where he was going or make any allusion to his return. He simply disappeared and reappeared when no one expected him to. There was nothing to make him suspect that this time was going to be different.

"You must help me!" Joy entreated when Mimmo called at the apartment on his way to work the day after Favour had left.

"*Calma!*" he reassured her.

"You have to get me out of here now before he comes back! This is my only chance to free myself, otherwise I'm doomed for ever."

Mimmo was confused and did not know what to do. He never liked being taken unawares. He liked to plan his course of action in advance and disliked the pressure that Joy was putting on him, but he knew he had to do something really quick. Without further procrastination he beckoned her to follow him. They both sneaked out of the apartment in great secrecy, as if the all-seeing eyes of Favour, who was a hundred kilometres away, were watching them.

"There's no time to waste. We must talk now that you're out of that horrible place." He tried to initiate a conversation with her as soon as they arrived in his studio flat in the heart of *Piazza Vittorio Emmanuele* in the nineteenth-century styled area of *Esquilino*. "Listen, you're safe here but not for too long. This is a central area, not far from the *stazione termini*. This is where you'll find most immigrants in this city. Many Nigerians have their businesses here, and many others come here to shop, send money home, or socialise. You can't hide in the midst of the same people you're trying to run away from."

Joy was not listening to him. She was engrossed with thoughts about her superficial newly found freedom. She was seeing some parts of the eternal city of Rome for the first time. She admired the architectural style of its imposing palazzo and its huge porticoes. She felt she was in Europe at last, and the last thought on her mind was the danger she was running away from.

"*Ascolta!*" Mimmo raised his voice, trying to get her attention to the harsh reality before them. He sensed from her excitement and the peaceful expression on her face that she had no clue about the dangerous situation she was in. She had found relative and temporary freedom at last. She had passed through the gates of hell and had caught a glimpse and indelible view of the devil himself. He was seated on his throne of evil and surrounded by his angels of darkness in the likes of Comfort, Mercy, Viktor, and Favour.

"Finally", she whispered quietly. The future looked bright and promising. She could at last begin to think of a decent job and earning an honest living. She could see herself through the eyes of the numerous immigrants she had sighted as she sat in front of a widescreen television. It was the biggest she had ever seen. It seemed as if they had nothing to do, other than to enjoy the freedom of life, thought, and expression that Europe had to offer, without any hassles or preoccupations. From the windows of Mimmo's flat she could see some of them preparing to pass the night in this largest Roman square, sleeping peacefully under the blue sky that was heavily populated by twinkling stars.

"Come, we must leave immediately. I'll explain things to you on the way. You must come with me now, or else you'll be sorry." He did not wait for her to understand or even ask questions. He dragged her vehemently and by the time she knew it, they were on the *Grande Racordo Anulare*, the orbital highway that encompassed the ancient city of Rome. "Here we are! At least you can now breathe freely and without fear for the next twenty-four hours."

"Where are we? Are we still in Rome?" She had slept like a baby all through the journey and was not aware that they had travelled close to two hours.

"This is *Terni*, my maternal home where I grew up. It's very safe here. My mum left me this massive property as her only child. At first I wanted to sell it, but all my childhood memories are here. I'd like to leave it to my children as their inheritance, but they have their own lives now. They don't like it here. They prefer the big cities like Roma, Firenze, and Bologna. I'm happy I still have this place. I come here occasionally when I really need a quiet place to stay and wind back time to replay my happiest memories."

"Wow! It's such a nice quiet place. I like it." One of Joy's greatest weaknesses was allowing her feelings of comfort and her false sense of security to becloud her judgement and her ability to perceive dangers. She had forgotten her plight all too soon. This was not a good sign for Mimmo. There was no time to waste. They had to have the most important conversation they would ever have.

"I am happy you're finally free from Favour's direct control, but being out of his flat doesn't mean that you're free at last. You must understand that you're even in a more dangerous situation now. He'll start looking for you as soon as he returns and discovers that you've left, and he'll do everything possible to find you. I won't tell you what that will mean for you. Those people are dangerous. They're criminals. They've got connections and informants all over the place, even in the police. They can find you wherever you hide because they think you owe them, and until you pay everything, you can't be completely free. Now you can understand the problem at hand. It's not as simple as you think. We must plan and think of a concrete way out."

"So what should we do?"

"I must tell you, it's not going to be easy at all. It's going to be a very long battle with possible casualties. There're so many things to put into consideration here. Let me try to break things down for you. Hiding away from the possible harm that Favour could inflict on you is just one side of the coin. For you to seek protection from the law, you must be legally resident. As things stand, you can't even go the police, no matter how life-threatening your situation is. Going to them would mean you're simply walking directly into the lion's den with your own two feet. They'll deport you immediately on the next available charter flight to Lagos, so that's completely out of the question."

Joy had no doubt that going to the police was no option. "So what else can I do? Maybe I can remain here with you and apply to stay legally. That way they'll not be able to come after me, and I'll have police protection."

"It's not as easy as you think. This is not Nigeria, where everything is possible as long as you have the money to pay for whatever you desire. Things are different here. You need to apply for the legal right of abode. It's the foreigners' stay permit called *permesso di soggiorno*, but you can only apply for this if and only if you already came in a legal way, so as you see, this too isn't your situation."

"I really can't understand. Surely there must be a way out. I don't think I'm the first person to come into the country illegally. Isn't there a place we can ask for help and more information?"

"Let me think. Yes, there might be another option. It's called *sanatoria*. It means amnesty in English. When you're amnestied, you're given an official pardon that allows you to live and work in Italy even if you've come in illegally."

"Bingo! That's it! When can I apply then?"

"Here you go again! You think everything is so easy! There's a clause that might change that happy expression on your face. The first bad news is that it's regulated by government legislation, so amnesties are rather sporadic. You can't tell when the next one's going to be. The second thing is that you have to be in employment when you apply. The thing is, nobody would want to employ you when you're an illegal immigrant, because they could be fined for breaking the law by employing those who are not regularised. Again, even if you're lucky enough to find employment, your employer will have to pay at least 1,000 euros as a contributory fee towards your regularisation. Many people shy from getting involved with immigrants because they cost money. Now tell me, who do you think would be ready to pay such money for a cleaner or *badante* who look after an elderly person for the miserable sum of five euros per hour?"

Joy did not know what to think. Every possible option seemed to come with its terms and conditions and insurmountable downsides that make it unappealing as a choice. "So where do I go from here? I can't go to the police, I can't apply for a *soggiorno,* and no one's ready to employ me. Meanwhile there are people out there waiting to take my life, and I can't do anything about it. Maybe I should just go back to where I'm coming from. Maybe Favour isn't back yet and has not discovered my absence. Even if he has, I can explain myself away and tell him I just stepped out for some fresh air."

"That's the only thing you must never do. They'll kill you and bury your body without anyone knowing about your demise. Remember that no one knows you're here. As far as the police are concerned, you don't exist in this country. You're not here, end of story, *finito.*"

"I'm so confused."

Mimmo had a final card to play in the interest of both of them, and this was the time to do so. "There's something I could do to make things easier for you. I'm going to do this as my own little way of showing repentance over the horrible things I've done to you. I know we met in compromising circumstances, but maybe that was destiny's way of bringing me into your life to help you. I couldn't have met you otherwise, or don't you think so?"

"Yes, you're right."

"Now listen to me. You already know me, and you know my story as well. I'm alone, in need of companionship, and you're equally alone, in need of documents to stay legally in this country. We can put our minds together and come to a mutual understanding and agreement."

For a moment Joy thought that he was proposing the old relationship—that he wanted to continue to sleep with her in exchange for accommodation, money, and protection. How could he be so mean? How could he even think of anything like that? Would it not be better to go to the police and be deported or even go back to Favour? Would this slavery and exploitation ever end? Why was it that everyone who encountered her only wanted the same thing?

"I can't believe that you pretend to want to help me, yet you're not in any way different from Favour and the rest of them. The answer is no to whatever you have in mind. I can't sleep with a man who's older than my father. I can't sleep with a man who pays money to sleep with a prostitute. I can't sleep with …"

"*Basta!*" Mimmo yelled instinctively in his native language. He could not believe that despite all the risk he had taken to bring her to safety, she did not trust him still. "You're getting it all wrong. I had something else in mind."

She blushed in shame and embarrassment. She had trusted everyone she should never have trusted and had doubted the only man who had showed her kindness and consideration. She did not want to give him too much credit by apologising. He still had too many sins to redress. She had come to understand one major thing about him: he never gave any explanation to unasked questions. "So what do you have in mind?"

"It's simple. Marry me."

This was even worse than she had thought. "What's the difference between sleeping with you and marrying you? So you think you're smart. You pretend to help, yet you're so selfish. What has marriage got to do with my quest to gain recognition as a legal immigrant?"

"If you let me, I'll explain the connection and why this option might be the only one workable in your personal circumstance." There was dead silence from Joy, so he understood that she was willing to hear him. "I'm Italian, and anyone I marry automatically becomes an Italian like me. You don't need any stay permit once you become a naturalised Italian by virtue of your marriage to me."

"*Tutto qui?* Is that all?"

"As simple as A-B-C. We can go to the *comune* right now and get it done." He knew deep in his heart that he was lying to her. He was not telling the whole truth. He had hidden the most important part of the information which would have made all the difference and made this option as unappealing as the others they had both previously considered. He lied about the terms and conditions attached to this offer. There was an incubation stage, a long and unspecified period of waiting, a limbo of transition between the heaven of becoming an adopted Italian and the hell of remaining clandestine. In the unlikely circumstance that Joy agreed to marry him in order to become an Italian, she would need to stay faithfully married to him for a period of at least two years before making claims to her new status. Two years was a long time for the unexpected to happen. There was also the question of her personal security. Her marriage to him would not be enough to shield her from the pending wrath of her traffickers. Mimmo knew and hid this fact. He prayed earnestly in his heart that she never asked any questions in that direction, and she did not—to his advantage and utter relief.

But it was not all about Joy. What was in it for him? He contemplated whether or not it was worthwhile to risk so much for a girl of her kind. Mimmo always saw the brighter side of life. He would finally have the chance to marry a brand new wife, approximately a quarter of his age. He would prove his virility to shame his ex-wife. He would be the envy of the little city of *Terni* as he went around town with his young bride, who was young enough to be his granddaughter. Most importantly, he would come clean with a sincere act of *mea culpa*. He would no longer need to go out in search of paid sex and feel like a dirty pervert. He would have his cake and eat it with apologies to no one. His old age would not be as lonely as he had often dreaded in the past.

Who knows? He might even father a child. Joy was in her prime youth. She might be desirous of one as time went by. Nothing would make him a happier man than fathering a *ciocolatino* from his Nubian queen.

The Joy who had been deceived into prostitution would have jumped up in celebration and believed everything she had just heard from the only trustworthy man in her universe, but the Joy who emerged victorious from two battles with death itself was slow to believe. Everyone around her had told her one lie or the other, starting with the lies of her auntie Comfort that landed her into a debt of 80,000 euros. There was Favour, who shamelessly confessed undying love and proposed to marry the same girl he had raped time over time again. She felt that Mimmo's proposal was too good to be true and needed to be investigated further.

"Just like that? Seriously? Do you mean to say that I'll automatically become an Italian if I agree to marry you?"

"*Semplicemente*. As simple as that. And there's even more to becoming my spouse. You'll no longer need to worry about any residence permit. You'll have free accommodation here in this villa and the studio apartment in *Piazza Vittorio Emmanuele* in Rome. Guess what? You won't even need to work or look for a job. I'll take care of all your needs. You can spend all day watching your favourite television programmes, and you can even buy some Nigerian Nollywood movies and watch them at your convenience. You can go shopping whenever and wherever you like. I'll also give you money to send to your parents every month. I'll give you clean money, not blood money from the Mafia or money from prostitution."

Joy saw herself in a daylight dream. She was afraid she would wake up to the tough reality facing her. She understood him perfectly well, but she wanted to be more than one hundred per cent sure that they were both on the same page. "Do you really mean everything you've just told me?"

"*Assolutamente!*" He could not be more convincing. "If you want, I can even add your name to the ownership documents of both properties and anyone of your choice if you so prefer. This one here is worth over 300,000 euros in the property market. It's all yours if you agree to marry me."

"Eureka!" She exclaimed silently in complete satisfaction. That was the incriminating catchy phrase she was looking out for. She knew he was up to something, but she found it hard to believe that he would go this far to make his blatant lie pass for the truth. She was uneducated but intelligent and not stupid either. How could a man ever give up all he had worked for in his entire life in exchange for a simple "I do" from a perfect stranger he had met just a few months back? Something kept telling her that this might well be another trap, but for now she had no choice. She needed more time to think and asked if he could drop the discussion until a later date and time, when she would have reflected well enough and be in a better frame of mind to make a well-informed decision.

"Take all the time you need, but not more than two weeks." Mimmo was very familiar with the fact that time in the African context was never measured but lived, that Africans were masters of their time, and that they had time for everything. For her, two weeks was time enough to gather evidence to prove his real intentions. Mimmo did not have to make recourse to the service of a magician or a soothsayer to make him realise that the next fortnight would be the most critical for him. He recognised that his words had not been enough to convince his would-be bride. He had to move to the next stage to back up his claims with concrete actions. For him, it was like going back to school at an age that was long past school age. The excitement was no longer there, but he had to make the best use of the short time ahead of him to woo the woman of the dream he never even knew he had.

# Chapter Eleven

The following two weeks were like heaven on earth for Joy. Mimmo made sure he left no stone unturned. He gave her a foretaste of what being married to him would be like. He treated her like a princess, and she felt like the Queen of Hearts. He brought her breakfast in bed or took her to the nearby bar for the best *cappuccino* and *cornetto* in the entire neighbourhood. They spent hours chatting about everything. They went to the nearby fruit and vegetable market to buy all they needed for a healthy dinner.

Mimmo knew the weakness of the majority of African men who frowned at domestic chores, and he used this to his greater advantage. He cooked for her while she sat there sipping orange juice. He cleaned the villa, ran the bath for her, took her shopping, and satisfied every one of her unexpressed desires. Joy felt as if she was touching the sky with the tip of a finger. She could not have been happier, even in a hundred years' time, with a man half his age. She forgot the age difference between them. Age was just a number, and you're as old as you feel, she consoled herself.

Mimmo had demonstrated the strength and character of a teenager in love, and he successfully passed the test with outstanding scores. Joy had made up her mind at the end of the two weeks that this was destiny in disguise. The only thing lacking was love, but Mimmo loved her, and that was all that mattered. She remembered her mother telling her that she should give preference to a man who loved her more than she loved him. Mimmo seemed to fit that category perfectly. She had to sacrifice something in order to enter into the wealthy place that a loveless marriage offered. "What's love got to do with it?" She remembered the famous song of Tina Turner. "After all, Mama didn't marry Papa for love. She didn't even marry him for money, she just married him as a man. I'm better off. I may not be marrying for love, but at least I'm definitely marrying for money. What's love without money anyway?" Life in Europe and the need to hold on to a reason to remain there had suddenly turned her into a Philosopher Queen–something she never knew she was.

It was the evening before she was to communicate her painstaking final decision to Mimmo, but he did not know this. For him, it was an evening like every other in the last weeks. He did not expect her to stick to the time deadline as a typical African, but she had decided to surprise him by doing just that in order to prove to him that she was both ready and able to live life in accordance with the dictates of a culture that was entirely different from hers. They had a fantastic romantic dinner. Her saving grace was her total abstinence from alcoholic drinks. His fatal enemy was the same alcohol, which played the timely role of an unexpected catalyst in what was inevitably bound to happen.

She had retired for the night when towards ten o'clock the unexpected happened. She found herself struggling with an unknown figure in the dark for the second time, but this time she would not accept defeat as an option. The woman who had lost the first battle without a fight was complacent, young, and naïve and had been brought to Europe under false pretences. The woman who was now lying on the bed would fight with the last drop of her blood. "Never again will a man take advantage of me," she had vowed after the encounter with Favour. She remembered the promise she had made to herself—that she would only give herself freely to the man who would finally put a ring on her finger. From her point of view this night was as important as her actual wedding night. It was the night before she finally planned to say yes to the man who had done everything possible to convince her that he was her husband of destiny. But now this man came in violently in the secrecy of the night to steal and to destroy what would have been his for ever if only he had been patient enough to wait a couple more hours.

She was in a total state of shock after she had freed herself from his clutches. He was too old and drunk to overpower the strength of a furious and overwhelmingly disappointed young woman. She ran as quickly as her legs could carry her and sprinted fearlessly out into the dark night. She kept on running for hours as if she was being chased by the Angel of Death himself. She ran until she was completely out of breath and strength. In resignation, she stopped to look back, only to discover to her amazement that no one was after her and that she was already in the outskirts of the city of Terni. She found herself staring directly into the face of an angel in white apparel and thought she was already dead and at the throne of judgement. She had always known that this day was going to come, but not this soon. As she stood before this angelic presence, her entire life flashed through her mind like a movie. She had died in sin; she had not had enough time to repent. Pastor Joshua had made her believe that she was saved, that only unbelievers who never accepted Christ as their Lord and Saviour in their lifetime would be liable to judgement, but here she was facing judgement even as a saved born-again Christian. She was her own judge. No one was there to condemn her, not even the angel, who simply stood there in silence without uttering a word. She was ready to spend eternity in the fires of hell. She had crossed the threshold and passed from life to death at the most inappropriate time, when she least expected it, when she was most unprepared for the encounter with the world beyond.

"My name is Sister Grace," said the angel dressed in white. "Don't worry, you'll be fine here with us. We picked you up from the streets two weeks ago. I'm happy you've gained consciousness. What's your name, young lady?"

"Two weeks ago? Picked up from the streets? Unconscious? Where am I?"

"You're in a hospital."

She was relieved to know that she was not dead. She was thankful for a second chance to put things in the right perspective. She vowed never again to be taken unawares. She had just been given the singular opportunity to return to life in the flesh after knocking at the closed gates of heaven.

Sister Grace belonged to a local Diocesan congregation in Nigeria. She had been appointed by the National Union of Catholic Nuns to assist in the work of rescuing, supporting, and reintegrating trafficked Nigerian women in Italy. She had attended an international conference on human trafficking organised by the American Embassy to the Holy See. During the conference she had had the opportunity to visit these modern-day slaves in their pitiable working conditions and environment. She was utterly traumatised and disheartened by what she saw. It was in no way comparable to the picture painted of this reality before then. Such pictures tended to focus on the gains and not the pains. The girls were not portrayed as the victims but as a greedy lot who freely signed a deadly contract with the devil to replicate Sodom and Gomorrah in these latter days. Her exposure to the reality of the street life of these girls was a life-changing encounter. She became a fierce advocate against the perpetuation of evil behind the trade of sexual slavery and exploitation. No girl in her right senses, she believed, would freely choose to live this way. She did not believe in the existence of free prostitution. "They are slaves, enslaved or entrapped," she often argued. "They're all coerced. They need to be liberated, even from their very own selves." As an indigene of Edo State, she felt particularly called to free her sisters. She had to forego a promising career in the religious life to restore these daughters of darkness to an image worthy of the primordial dignity and identity of Idia, the historical Queen Mother of Edo Land. Between her naturally driven passion to restore the tarnished image of womanhood and her divine vocation to seek and save the lost, Sister Grace could not tell which was her stronger motivation. Rather than fight from the home front, she had opted for a full immersion into the front line itself. Her vision was to remove every girl of black skin colour from the streets of Italy.

She was both consoled and thankful when Joy finally came out of her two-week long coma. It was the beginning of a very long journey, but she had all the necessary patience and much more. She believed that the journey of a thousand miles starts with one first step, and that Rome was indeed not built in a day.

Joy was discharged from the hospital shortly after she woke up. She had sustained no internal injury of any kind. She was only in an acute state of shock, and a fortnight's rest was all she required to recuperate. Fortunately, she had suffered no memory loss. She was immediately driven away to a *prima accoglienza*, a first reception safe house, where she could feel safe and protected enough to reflect and decide on the way forward.

Sister Grace would not take her final leave until she had mentioned some of the ground rules, which must strictly be adhered to. "You'll be here for two weeks or a bit more, but it's a temporary accommodation. I'll need to go back to my community now, but I will come for you sooner than you expect. Remember that these sisters are only helping you out of their own free will and the love they have for God. To them you're still a perfect stranger, so make sure you follow their rules. You must not use a mobile phone or attempt to get in contact with anyone, not even members of your family. This is the first and most important rule that you mustn't break. Then you must respect meal time and prayer time routine; these are not optional but obligatory. One last thing. This is a place of prayer and silence, and these sisters don't speak English, so you don't have to bother yourself trying to communicate with them. Keep all your questions until my return. I'm sure you can survive these two weeks considering where you're coming from and what's happened to you."

She made for the door and slowly disappeared as she spoke, leaving Joy all alone to face the greatest challenge in a world of frightening and deafening silence. Sister Grace returned as promised. She knew it was deliberation and decision time. She went directly to the point. "You now have to make a decision after considering the options available to you. Unfortunately, you don't' have much time to do this, but listen. Basically, you can decide to return to your country of origin or you can decide to remain here and be re-integrated in this country."

Joy could not believe that the nun could even think of her going back home. Her countenance betrayed her feelings, but Sister Grace had been through this before. Few girls considered the option of returning home. They did not want to be stigmatised or return empty-handed after they had gone through hell to get away. She knew exactly how Joy felt, but as a matter of protocol she had to let her know what the option really involved, regardless of her choice.

"If you decide to go home, know that you can choose to return to your family or another city of your choice where no one knows you and where you can start life all over again. You can decide to return to school or to start a small-scale business of your choice. You won't be alone. There are inter-governmental and non-governmental organisations that will help you to return home, offer you protection, and support you in whatever you decide to do. Apart from paying for your flight, they'll give you money to pay for your school fees or to start a business." That sounded pretty good to Joy. Sister Grace needed all her diplomatic skills in order to proceed further. It was the right time to appeal to her value system. "My dear, you should know it's not always about money. Think about your dignity and the pride you will feel in returning victorious to your country after your ordeal. You should consider yourself a hero, someone exceptional, a role model who'll inspire others to turn their backs on the dangers of being trafficked."

Her words fell on deaf ears. Joy could not make sense of any discussion that centred on dignity, pride, or identity. They were words that had long been deleted from her vocabulary. Everything now for her was about money, and she needed to streamline their discussion just around that. "Thank you, but no."

"If you decide to remain here, you'll also need to know what you're signing on for. If you decide to return to Nigeria, I can assure you that all this will happen within one month, but if you decide on the contrary, things may not move as quickly. In fact, I don't know how long it will take for you to be fully integrated, that is, if you ever will be. You really need to listen attentively." Joy was silent, and Grace assumed that she was listening closely. "If you choose to go back to Nigeria, you'll be doing yourself a whole lot of good. You won't need to disclose the identity of your trafficker to the police; you'll only need to go to the Nigerian High Commission to obtain an emergency travelling certificate. No person alive or dead would know what has happened to you. But if you decide to stay, you'll need to disclose all you know about the people who tricked you into prostitution. It is considered a crime here, so the government will only think of allowing you to stay in exchange for the information you give them to help them track down and fight criminals who traffic young girls for sexual exploitation. And that's not all …" Joy was beginning to show signs of distress and discomfort, so Sister Grace sensed it was time to take a break. "Would you care for a cup of tea or a cold drink? We can continue later if you want."

Joy wanted to hear it all at once. "I'm fine, Sister. Just carry on."

"Once you've revealed their names, Interpol will begin an investigation to corroborate your story to determine if you told the truth or not and whether the information you've given is useful to them. If not …"

"So they can refuse my stay? How's that possible?" She felt entrapped on both sides. If she decided to go back home, her life would be in danger, and if she decided to remain, some other person's life would be in danger as well. Comfort and her cohorts could be arrested, but what would happen after their jail term? What if they did not get arrested at all? She did not even know her whereabouts, so how could she convince the police that she was telling the truth? Her mind went swiftly to Mercy and Favour. All she remembered about Mercy was that she lived in Torino and made her the most delicious *spaghetti alla Bolognese* she ever had. Favour lived somewhere off *via Casilina*. The only detail she remembered about the vicinity was the bus top, which the girls renamed *ashawo bus stop* as there was always a Nigerian street worker to be found waiting for a bus at that particular station at any time of the day or night. Now that she started to think about these details, she knew there were terms used by the girls to describe places and people that the Italian police would find difficult to understand or locate.

"Yes, they can refuse your case and say it's not genuine. There are girls who want to remain but are afraid to reveal the true identity of their traffickers. These girls give false names, and the Italian police are aware of this possibility. You can't have your cake and eat it too. If you've decided to remain, then you must collaborate with them to get what you want."

Joy needed a change of topic. She did not want to dwell further on this, as she needed more time to decide. However, Sister Grace continued, hoping not to be interrupted for a while.

"Once you've decided to stay and have gone through with the preliminary interview with the police, you'd need to come with me to the Nigerian High Commission to be identified as a Nigerian. They'll issue you a certificate of nationality, and with this document I'll take you to the *Questura,* the office that handles and issues *permesso di soggiorno* or residence permits for foreigners. This may all sound easy and simple, but you really need to be very patient. This is Italy, and the bureaucracy is very peculiar. Let's put it this way. You know when you start, but never know when it will end—if it will ever end at all. And finally …" Joy sighed in great relief that this conversation was gradually coming to an end, at least for the day. "We'll need to find you another accommodation, one that is permanent, depending on whether or not you qualify to remain by obeying the rules and regulations. But that's a story for another day."

Sister Grace had to take her leave. She was heading directly to the nearest police station to report Joy's case and open a case file. Joy had one last request to make before that. She had been away from home for more than a year. She wanted to find out how her family was. She particularly missed her mother and wanted to find out if Comfort had showed up or threatened her family since her escape, only a month ago. She had passed the initial test of not making use of the phone for the first two weeks. Now Sister Grace had no choice but to oblige her, but she wished she didn't have to.

"Mama, it's me, Joy. Can you hear me? It's me, Mama. How's Papa?"

Her mother had been waiting for this day to come. She had almost lost hope, and now that it was finally here and she could hear her daughter's voice again, she knew there was no time for a frivolous exchange of pleasantries.

"Don't come back! You must do everything not to come back if you don't want to die like your father. Your auntie Comfort has been threatening all of us here. She told us stories that you rebelled and ran away from the job she found for you and that you're now a bad girl. She said she had paid money to sponsor your travel and that your father should pay her back. He refused, and next thing we find him dead in a very mysterious way. I'm so confused. I'm sorry to put you through all this, but please do all you can not to return home."

At that point the mobile phone ran out of credit. Joy was petrified by what her mother had just told her. What other price was she expected to pay? She had lost a kidney, her virginity, and now her father. There was now no second thought about the outcome of her day-long discussion with the Roman Catholic nun. The handwriting on the wall was clear enough even for a blind man.

Joy was housed with the community of sisters of *Madonna della Nigrizia*, a missionary group that had worked predominantly in African countries, especially in Kenya and Uganda, with their motherhouse in Rome. They decided to offer accommodation to support trafficked women since their numbers had decreased drastically due to fewer women having a vocation to the religious life and a reduction in the number of African missions requiring expatriates. They also received and accommodated young women from Albania, Romania, Moldavia, and Russia, but the majority were from Nigeria with a handful from Ghana. Joy was received into the community after her initial deposition with the police. This had been more of a cross examination, as they used every means at their disposal to make her admit that she came to Italy of her own free will and was lying deliberately about being trafficked as a way of regularising her otherwise illegal status. She had been solemnly initiated into what was going to be her new life over the next couple of years or so during the first two weeks she had earlier spent in first reception. Her stay in this new community was not much different, except for the noise level of her current abode, which was acceptably "normal".

While silence had been the greatest challenge in her previous accommodation, boredom had now become her number one concern. In the previous situation, she knew the duration of her stay, but this time she had no clue just how long her Calvary was going to last, and this made it even more agonising. On a typical day, she would wake up in the ungodly hour of five o'clock when most of the city of Rome was still asleep. She would recite the breviary in the Italian language with the nuns, followed by mass, celebrated by a supply student priest from the nearby *collegio*. They would then all proceed in a single file to the refectory for a scanty breakfast of some dried, tinned, or fresh fruits donated by a neighbouring supermarket just before or shortly after the sell-by date. As much as she tried, Joy found it extremely hard to comprehend why they always had to eat their breakfast in silence and in a hurry, as if they were getting ready for a modern re-visitation of the Jewish Passover or were mourning some imminent but unannounced death. Lunch was a more light-hearted encounter. A bell rang at some point after a short reading from *The Imitation of Christ* by Thomas à Kempis to lift the ban from silence that had been imposed since the previous night's bedtime. Often the girls preferred the silence, because some of the questions asked by some of the aged Italian nuns were somewhat embarrassing and thought-provoking.

"Is it true that people still live in trees in Africa?" eighty-eight year old Suor Lucia would unfailingly ask at lunchtime. She suffered from dementia and Alzheimer's disease, a medical condition that excused what the girls saw as a form of "polite insult" and "whitewashed racism".

"And we do not eat with our own five fingers," the girls would echo in unison. They knew exactly what question would follow.

The most mind-numbing times of the day were in-between meals. The girls became literally jobless after they had rushed through their allocated daily chores. The nuns had, without much success, introduced some basic skills acquisition such as sewing, knitting, jam-making, and gardening. The girls never saw the usefulness of this time-consuming initiative. They particularly detested the weekly Italian language lesson, taught by a retired Spanish volunteer. All they ever wanted was to work and earn some money for themselves rather than queue to ask and be refused. Joy had not been long in this establishment before she began to feel the crunch of missing Nigerian cuisine.

"Three years? You've been here for this long? Why? Doing what?" Joy was as curious as much as she was anxious.

The girls had been instructed. They knew the type of conversation that they must never be involved in with a new guest. "You might be lucky. Your case might be different," they would reply, dismissing her and avoiding getting themselves into trouble.

# Chapter Twelve

Sister Grace turned up one morning. She had come to accompany Joy to the Nigerian High Commission, located within the vicinity of the Vatican City. Joy had never seen so many co-nationals together in one single place. The Nigeria House reminded her of Oba Market in Benin City. There were different ethnic groups speaking a variety of local Nigerian languages and dialects like Yoruba, Ibo, Urhobo, and Edo, her own native tongue. They had come from different cities. Some had spent the night in their cars, and others travelled on an all-night train, just to ensure they would be seen on the day. They had come for different reasons, including change of name, age, or status, *nulla osta* for marriages, certificates of nationality, and passport renewal or re-issue. The premises of the High Commission was jam-packed as early as eight o'clock as some settled for a packed breakfast while others bought food and snacks from vendors. Business went on both inside and outside the premises. Touts operated with impunity, shamelessly offering their middleman services for cut-throat fees, exploiting the computer illiteracy, ignorance, and sheer laziness of their co-nationals without pity for their pockets.

It was 11.45 when the Consular Officer finally made his appearance like a warrior fully armed for battle. He was very unapproachable and unfriendly. Nigerians meeting him for the first time had the impression they were in for big trouble simply for being unfortunate enough to have been born in that part of the world. People dreaded any form of encounter with the "madman" as both local staff and service users called him. He was always angry about something, with someone, or even with himself for being posted to this office. He had previously worked in the United Kingdom and the United States of America, where he was known to be very diligent in the disposition of his consular duties. He was always ready to help. He was overly ambitious as a career diplomat and had to prove his worth in order to get the promotion and enviable posting that was more likely to be handed on a platter of gold to undeserving political diplomats simply because of their affiliations and connections to the powers that be. He was known to always go the extra mile to help a co-national with genuine problems that he was able to handle in his position and power.

Contrary to the endearing personality he had demonstrated in former assignments, his posting to Italy revealed some traits in his character that were hitherto unknown even to him. He always wore an angry look. He was highly irritable, explosive, aggressive, impolite, and verbally abusive. No one really bothered to find out why Italy had transformed a lamb into an angry and roaring lion that was always on the lookout for someone to devour. He had always believed that it was only the worst breed of Nigerians without dreams and aspirations that found their way to Italy. He struggled to understand why his co-nationals came to a country that had nothing to offer them. It vexed him even more that his co-nationals who flooded the cities of Italy were as hopeless and helpless as the host country with its history of massive youth unemployment, stagnant growth in infrastructure, prolonged economic crisis, and laughable political system. As one with a passionate love for literature in all its forms and expressions, he was particularly thrilled by *The Canterbury Tales* of Geoffrey Chaucer. He disliked Nigerians who claim to have earned doctorate degrees from various state and pontifical universities in Italy yet were unable to make simple complete sentences in English without corruption by its Italian tinge. He got mad over the simple wrong use of prepositions and bad grammar, especially verb tenses. He hated it when he asked a simple and straightforward question like "What's your name?" and received responses like "My names are Doctor ..." "Fool!" he would scream uncontrollably. "You don't even understand simple English. I'm asking for your name. and you're giving me a litany of names. By the way, is 'Doctor' your name too? You don't even know the difference between a name and a title. Did your Mama name you 'Doctor' when you were born? Just get out of my office and come back when you can behave and talk like someone living abroad." He had spoken, and his final words always prevailed.

"Come with me, Sister Grace," the Consular Officer said after scanning through the heads of his co-nationals who had been sitting in the waiting area all morning. He had immediately spotted the nun's veil. She was the only person who had been thoughtful enough to make an appointment. Others simply turned up with their myriads of complicated issues, waiting for them to be magically resolved. For all he cared, they could wait for eternity. "So you've brought me another face of shame and disgrace to our dear country—the same old cock-and-bull story, another girl. Young girl," the Officer switched from the nun to Joy without warning, "please save your pitiable and disgusting story for those who are stupid enough to buy it, not me. I know your type, and I can't believe that the Federal Government of Nigeria sent me here to waste my time on infidels like you. If you really need my help, you must at least tell me the truth. I hate lies and I hate liars even more. You must at least admit that you came here voluntarily to do *ashawo* work. Do yourself a big favour and don't give me that crap story that you were deceived into it. No! Not after almost two decades of the same old lie!"

Sister Grace knew exactly what was going to happen. She knew the officer too well to think that he would not give up before he achieved his purpose of extracting some form of confession, even under duress. "Sir, please take it easy. She's been through a lot, and I can personally assure you that her case is genuine."

"Like all the others, Sister. I know you would even vouch for the devil himself just to save him. You know what, Sister? You encourage these girls by helping them. If you left it up to me, they'd all be in the next charter flight for Lagos."

The Consular Officer had seen how many people were waiting to see him. He did not want to waste his precious time on this case. He knew that Sister Grace would never leave without the document she had come for. He therefore called his secretary and gave the go-ahead for the certificate of nationality to be issued in favour of Joy Osaro. He thought that he had successfully handled his first case for the day, but Sister Grace had not made all the painstaking effort to book an appointment just for one singular case.

"Sir, I'm still waiting to receive feedback about the forty-nine girls whose passport applications are still pending. You know their case very well, Sir. They came in with passports that were not issued in their names. Now they've given their real names and identities to the Italian police. This office issued the initial certificate of nationality in their real names, and with these we've been able to get the *questura* to issue a first-stay permit in their real names. The problem is that they need valid passports with their own names before renewing their stay permits. You see, sir, we really need these passports, otherwise, the *questura* won't renew their permits. It now depends entirely on this office whether these girls are to be fully integrated or not. Please help us, sir. We've got barely six months before the expiration of the first permits. Please, sir, help!"

"Sister, things are not as easy as you think. We've told you that the first thing you'll need to do is to pay for the cost of each passport, which is 300 euros. Unfortunately, we can't close an eye and encourage these girls to continue to come here to disgrace us by issuing them free passports. For normal co-nationals with genuine cases and an old existing passport booklet issued in their real names with a valid entry visa, the cost for reissue is sixty-five dollars, but the case of your girls is quite different. The cost is 300 euros, and this is non-negotiable. This is the High Commission, not a charitable organisation founded by Mother Theresa."

"Sir, things have changed since the last time I visited this office. The problem is no longer the money. Various associations have donated generously, and we've made all payments. Well-meaning citizens have raised the sum of 14,700 euros paid to this office, which, by the way, should show some solidarity by issuing these passports free of charge for humanitarian reasons. But the reason for my anger is that these passports are nowhere to be found, even after we'd made such huge payments, I went personally to the High Commissioner who said the cases are being handled in Abuja, the headquarters. I've been to Abuja too, and they told me to come back here. With all due respect, this is becoming embarrassing. What do we tell those who raised the money? This is both unfair and unfortunate. People talk of these girls as being exploited and—I don't mean to be rude here—even this Office is not doing anything different. How can they accept such huge amounts of money without bothering to issue the required documents? This is fraud! Give us the passports or have the decency to refund the money!"

"Calm down, Sister. You don't need to insult this office indirectly as if we're not doing our job. We can't solve all problems here. We have to refer some to headquarters or even to Interpol. The problem is that people come here believing we've got the power and ability to work miracles. Now listen, the main problem now is the transition to the new biometric passports. These new passports carry fingerprints and bio data which can't be changed once issued. These girls can't receive new passports as their fingerprints are already on the system with all relevant data they gave as at the time. Now that can't be changed. You'll remember that when we had the old non-biometric passports we had no problems changing names, details, and so on. This is no longer possible with the new biometric passports. They are designed to avoid duplication and abuse. With the old passports, it was possible for a national to have multiple passports in different names. With the new ones it's strictly one passport per person."

"So what's the conclusion then?"

"There's no alternative. They've got to stick to their old passports and bear those names."

"You forget one detail, sir. They don't have those passports. They've been taken away from them. You might not understand this, sir, but the very first step towards reintegrating these girls is getting hold of their own identity without which they're lost, invisible, and non-existent."

"Unfortunately, there isn't much I can do for now, Sister. I'm really sorry, but I need to attend to others now. Please wait in the hall while my secretary prepares to hand you the certificate of nationality for the girl. We'll talk about the other cases some other time. Just keep praying. You believe in miracles, don't you? Thanks again for coming, and excuse me once again."

He politely saw them out through the door. Joy had digested every bit of the conversation between the nun and the Consular Officer. She had just been issued a certificate of nationality, but that only made her case similar to the near-hopeless situation of the forty-nine passport applicants before her. She had heard more than enough to know that even in the most unlikely situation that she were issued with the first-stay permit for the duration of one year, it was most improbable that it would be renewed, as had just been confirmed by the Consular Officer. "What happens to me after that? Will I have to go back to the streets? Will the reverend sisters continue to harbour me if I have no legal documents to remain? Would they not be breaking the law? Am I really worth this much?" She had so many questions and no answers in sight. She had accepted the offer of the nun because she believed she could help her to regularise her stay. For some time now, the discussion about getting a job, which was the reason why she agreed to travel, had become secondary as she could not work without a legal right of abode. The primary priority of getting a stay permit was no longer as guaranteed as it had first sounded.

Her visit to Nigeria House had been memorable for a multiplicity of reasons. She had, for the first time in a long while, heard people speaking her dialect in a strange land. For once she felt that she was not alone and was part of the wholeness of humanity. This gave her reason to hope for survival, though it was entirely dependent on her obtaining a legal right of abode—a dream unknowingly nipped in the bud by the revelations of that irritatingly unforgettable Consular Officer, who like the madman in Fredrick Nietzsche's *Thus Spake Zarathustra*, announced the death of God.

Joy needed tranquillity to take in this new information and decide the next step to take without making an error in judgement. The more she thought it through, the more she became entangled in a web from which she felt she could never be completely liberated for a long time to come. Ironically, she seemed to find herself exactly at the same point of departure just when she was beginning to think that she had found the right solution once and for all to her enigmatic situation.

Her mind went back in a flash to Mimmo and the preposterous life he had offered her without batting an eyelid. She wondered if she had been too quick to judge and too naïve to see the bigger picture. After all, life is always about compromise. She thought that she could turn back time, return to him, and pick up exactly from where they had stopped. "It was only the work of the devil. He was under the influence of alcohol. I'm sure he must be repentant and sincerely remorseful by now. That really wasn't him, even if he wasn't drunk. I should have been more patient. Didn't Papa rape Mama time after time after spending his entire day drinking at the local beer parlour in the company of his lazy, lousy, and jobless friends?" She could not help but compare her own father to Mimmo, a man who was more than a million times better in every sense of the word. He was rich, caring, and loving and offered her more than she could ever wish for, unlike her father who forcibly took advantage of her mother in exchange for nothing except the bonus of appending the title "Mrs" to her name. "All women are bound to be raped at one time or the other, for different reasons, by different men, depending on how they are interpreted by the same women." She consoled herself in philosophical justifications. She was now convinced that she had made a fatal error to have escaped from the dangerously protective arms of the fatherly Mimmo. Whatever the case may be, it was too late now. She had missed the unique train to the fulfilment of destiny, and there was no going back. She could not, even if she had wanted to. She did not know how or where to find him. It was not meant to be, otherwise there would have been a point of contact such as a telephone number or an address. It was as if he never existed, and there was nothing she could do about it other than to let sleeping dogs lie.

The visit to the High Commission was the catalyst that she so much needed in order to come to the realisation that the reintegration plan was not an option for her. There must be a way out, she told herself. As a Nigerian, she knew that there was a solution to every problem. The only issue was finding the right contact, and the rest would be history. She was absolutely sure to pay a return visit to Nigeria House sooner rather than later. She had seen other girls who seemed to be in a situation similar to hers. She was sure that was the right place to start, and this time around she was more than certain that her instinct would not disappoint her. She wrote a farewell note. She hated saying goodbyes.

Dear Sisters,

If you're reading this note, it means I'm already gone, never to return. Please don't look for me, as I've gone in search of my own destiny. I'll never forget your hospitality. Thanks for all your help, and sorry for any inconvenience my stay may have caused you.

Yours in Christ.

Joy.

She made her way to the High Commission in the earliest hours of the next day. When she had visited with Sister Grace on the previous day, she had spotted a young girl in her early twenties. She was well dressed and looked confident, happy, and independent. Above all, she exhibited no sign of stress and seemed to be in absolute control of herself as one who did not have to be accountable to anyone for any reason whatsoever. Joy's instinct was that she was the right contact. Her instinct also told her that this same girl was most likely to be in the High Commission the next morning. She was not wrong.

"You've done the right thing. I came back here because I felt you'd need my help. I knew you'd be back this morning, and that's exactly why I'm here, Oh! Excuse my manners. I'm Charity."

"Charity?" Joy exclaimed in utter surprise and relief. That name sounded all too familiar. It reminded her of the Charity with whom she had travelled from Benin City to the Island of Lampedusa before she lost sight of her. She wondered where she was now and hoped she was there to encourage her with her wild ideas. Here right in front of her was another person with the same name, trying to be of help to her exactly like the other. Maybe this was her guardian angel, sent to lead her finally on the right path.

"I'm Joy." She struggled to speak. Her mind was still full of reflections about her experience in transit with Peace and Charity.

"You don't need to tell me your story. I was in the same situation as you, and you've done the most courageous thing you could do. In your situation it's very easy to trust people who pretend they're there to help you, but you should know that you're the only person who can really help yourself. No one else will. Don't mind them. Money, the right amount of money, can work any miracle. They know that the reverend sisters aren't about to pay bribes. If not, they shouldn't be meeting with him in the first place. Again, that 'madman' of an officer is so impatient and angry as if it's now a crime against humanity to come from *Naija*. You see, if you approach him directly, then he is forced to behave officially and speak big grammar because he knows there's nothing there for him. You'd be surprised how the story will change when money begins to change hands at the back gate."

"I can't believe what I'm hearing."

"And that's not all. Sister Grace will keep coming and going until the officer finishes his term of office. Then everything has to start again from the scratch. It's either a change of officer or the high commissioner himself, and that changes everything and increases waiting time. They just keep frustrating you until you decide to forget about the problem that brought you here in the first place or live with it as if it never existed."

"This is all very confusing."

"Don't worry, you've met the right person. Let me start by shocking you. Do you know that a *kpali* is not really the first thing you need?"

"What?"

"Yes, it only identifies you as a Nigerian. It doesn't give you the right of abode. It's only useful for you to apply for a *soggiorno*. It doesn't prevent you from being deported if the police catch up with you. So you see, this document doesn't carry all that much weight and importance."

Joy had never heard anything more shocking and illuminating. This was the first rational conversation she had had since her arrival. Everyone else had tried to tell her partial truths without making her see the whole picture. They only revealed the necessary bits that served to reassure her, when in reality her underpants were on fire.

"I know you're a smart girl, so let me tell you things you'll never read in the books. I'm doing this completely free of charge. It's big stuff, a real load of knowledge that even graduates from Oxford University don't know. That's why they call me Madame Philosopher."

"Madame? Aren't you too young for that?"

"Yes, but it's just a way of recognising that I'm big, not old. Anyway just call me Philosopher. I know all you need to know, in black and white, without additions or subtractions. I'm the body of knowledge. Now, let's get back to real talk." Nothing pleased Charity better than a flamboyant demonstration of how much she knew. "That's not the ideal, but unfortunately it's the reality. And the bitter truth is that you might think that you're okay with six euros an hour, but where does that leave you if you have to pay all your bills by yourself like gas, electricity, *nettezza urbana, condominio,* and water, not to mention food and clothing? Your take-home every month from a cleaning job won't go beyond 400 euros, but you'll need a minimum of 900 euros to survive. The larger chunk goes for your rent, which is fifty per cent, not counting the money you'll need to remit monthly to your family and dependants. Do you want me to continue?"

"I never thought of it that way before. This is becoming a real nightmare. Where's it all going to end?"

"Most of them go back to what you and I know well. It still remains the fastest way of making money out here. Then again, instead of thinking only about what comes in, you can also save on what goes out. For example you can save huge sums of money on transportation and food. Most foreigners don't pay bus or train fares, and you can't blame them. The system encourages such practices. Then again, you can eat freely from the many *mensas* of *caritas*. Even the Italians themselves now eat at these free places because of the recession and hard-hit economy. They even collect clothing items too." Charity casually glanced at her imitation Gucci watch and discovered they had been talking close to two hours. "Enough with the talking. It's time for action. I'll take you to someone who'll clear all your doubt and confirm that all I've told you is the undiluted truth."

# Chapter Thirteen

Avvocato Carpisa was a famous name and face among the immigrant community in Rome. He shuttled between several African Embassies, including the Nigerian High Commission. He also operated his business from a consultancy room in the centre for temporary detention of illegal migrants in *Ponte Galeria*. It was usual for him to visit places of mass African agglomerations such as the open market at *Piazza Vittorio Emmanuele*. He also attended exclusive Church events such as baptism, confirmation, and first communion, strictly by personal invitation as a highly visible and honourable humanitarian. He often defined himself not as an African but an Africanist, one who was fortunate enough not to be born with black skin or on the Dark Continent but who nevertheless had the aims and interests of Africa and her people at heart. He prided himself on being happily married to a woman who never identified with him or his interests. He also claimed to have the two most wonderful adolescent daughters. However, he had never been spotted even once in the company of his enviable family. The only fact that could be validated about him was that his celebrity-like wedding was celebrated by a top Vatican watchdog in the prestigious and historical basilica of St Mary of the Angels and the Martyrs. Superficially, he was a practising Roman Catholic to the core, a position he gainfully exploited as a cover-up for his dreadfully shady deals. Although he came across as a meticulous, fast-thinking, and passionate lawyer who always delivered and was never known to have lost a case, his dark side revealed him as unethical. His only concern was money. He often professed to work exclusively in the interests of the girls, freely as a charity lawyer who was serving the public interest in the plight of the girls.

Avvocato Carpisa had a secret that was unknown even to his wife and adorable family. He was a drop-out from the University of Rome. He was smart enough to fake a profession he knew nothing about, and he convinced people that he was not only good but great at what he did. He was everything except the advocate he claimed to be. Ironically, this was the best he did.

"*Buon giorno avvocato!*" Charity greeted him as she stepped into his consultation room in *Ponte Galeria*, with Joy sluggishly following behind.

He returned her greetings with half a smile, pointing at the two empty seats in front of him. It had been a terrific day for him. He was working on the appeal cases against the immediate deportation order of twenty Nigerian girls. He had only a few hours left to conclude these very difficult cases, and he needed no distractions at all. Once he had completed all the paperwork, he was sure of taking home the sum of 20,000 euros in cash. He knew his job all too well. He knew the right buttons to press, the right palms to grease, and the right documents to put forward so that his clients would be as free as the wind to blow wherever they liked.

"Girls, you really have to wait for me to finish this. I'll be with you shortly."

Three hours later, he exhaled with sheer relief and gratification. He had just concluded some exceptionally outstanding deals with no tax attached. Here was another one sitting right in front of him. The day could not be proceeding in a better way. He was skilled at his job, which he had come to master through constant practice, astuteness, and hard work. No formal qualification would have given him the kind of skills he had come to master on this job as second nature. He knew his clientele so well. He had spent so much time in the company of Africans that he enjoyed the best of both worlds. He had come to learn from experience that money was not the first item to be discussed under such circumstances; he had to make the case look as hopeless and impossible as he could and then narrow it down to his role as saviour and only possible solution.

"I must be very frank with you. I'm an Italian, and I know the laws of my country both as a person and a legal practitioner. You can only come into this country as a worker, as a student, or for a family reunion. Let me state straight away that no one actually gets a visa to come to this country as a worker, because this means you must have found a job even before you come in, so that option is completely out. The second option is to come in as a student. I don't think that is your case. The third option is to come in to join your spouse, and this too is not your case. Now you have come in without any valid reason or document to prove it. This means you have broken the laws of this country and you're liable to punishment. You can be deported and won't be allowed to return for ten years. But I can help you remain and avoid being deported. To do this, I must find a valid reason."

Both girls were completely silent. Charity knew exactly where the lawyer was going and restrained Joy from asking questions that would only serve to prolong their visit that was already too long.

"*Si, avvocato*, just go ahead and tell her what she needs to do. I'm sure you want to go home early to your beloved family after such a hectic day."

"To be honest, your friend here has no reason whatsoever to remain, but I can invent one for her, don't worry." Avvocato Carpisa spent the next half hour explaining the procedure of applying for political asylum as a Liberian. He made it quite clear that this was only a strategy to gain time, knowing fully well that the process was quite leisurely and could take up to three years or more. "This means you have at least three years to live and work in this country without harassment and fear of deportation. All you need to do is to make sure that you keep your application slip with you all the time. With this you can apply for a *gratuito patroncinio*, which allows you free access to some essential services, and you can also use all the free services offered by *Caritas* and go about your business of making money, or isn't that what you came here for?"

Joy felt happier after hearing that there was the possibility of remaining for a period of three years or more. Her American dream came alive for a moment before Carpisa made his final remarks.

"I've left the most important part of this conversation out until now, but there's a need for clarity in order to avoid misunderstanding. I know you've got no money on you, but you'll understand that there is a fee for all I'm about to do for you. I don't want you to worry about that now. I'm sure you'll know how to show due appreciation when the time comes."

Joy had heard those same words before from Barrister Bright in Benin City. The appreciation he referred to then was later translated into a debt of 80,000 euros with Comfort. She had found a ray of light and hope, but she had no idea what "appreciation" to Avvocato Carpisa would amount to. She was clear about one thing: she had put herself further in debt. The thought of owing money to so many people without any apparent reason was confusing to her. Everyone seemed to want her to pay back some money, yet she had no income of her own. All she had heard so far was how much she had to pay to secure the permit to live in a country she did not choose. Why was no one talking about a job? What kind of job could she do to pay off all these accumulated debts? Carpisa had just made reference to the "business of making money", and she did not need any interpreter to explain this. She had just been given free licence to prostitute without the fear of prosecution. "Welcome to Italy," she said to herself, as she made up her mind once and for all to face up to what had been revealed as her true destiny from which she could no longer run away.

She went back home with Charity after their encounter with the lawyer. Charity lived in a tiny room in a three-bedroom apartment that she shared with two other girls in *via casilina*. Joy still remembered the route of bus 105 that she had used when she was under the bondage of Favour, the man who claimed to love her but stole the most precious thing she ever had, like a thief in the night. It had been a long day, and she was too tired to show any excitement about her newfound freedom. It was the first time that she had been welcomed by a friend. She felt happy, peaceful, and relaxed. She fell asleep on the two-seat sofa in the sitting room as Charity hurried to the kitchen to quickly find something for them to share before going to bed.

When she woke up, it was past eight o'clock the next morning. She was surprised at herself that she slept that long. The nuns' wake-up bell was not there to interrupt her sleep at five o'clock and call her to morning prayers, followed by mass and a silent breakfast and a day spent in total monotony. Joy did not want to get too comfortable with her brand-new liberty until she knew what it would cost her. She had been indebted times without number without knowing it, and she had been expected to pay exorbitantly for her bondage. She wondered what the price of this independence would be. She made up her mind to have a discussion with her host as soon as she woke up about the terms and conditions of her hospitality. If there was something she was not prepared for, it was plunging herself into what she was not ready for.

Charity had travelled this road before and was not surprised when Joy expressed her fears about her stay. She knew she had gone through enough for her not to trust anyone who tried to be of help to her. She knew from experience that the only person to be doubted was, ironically, the true and unconditional helper that she was trying to be. The only way she could prove her genuineness was to let her into her own world by sharing her own story.

"I belonged to the choir in my church. I had just got admission into the university to read Mass Communication. I love everything about information technology, and my dream is to become the first female minister of Communication and Information Technology. Things took a drastic turn when my pastor came up with a proposal that I thought was the best thing that could ever happen to a girl with my kind of dreams and aspirations. He said I would travel with a female diplomat on her first posting to Italy to take care of her children, in exchange for a university education abroad. I was unbelievably excited. I never believed I could travel abroad. When I finally arrived here, the story was completely different. I became a domestic slave to the same person who had promised to send me to the university. She received allowances to pay for a baby sitter, a cook, a cleaner, and a gardener, but she made me to do all the work and paid me no money. But that wasn't all. My greatest problem was her husband. He was unemployed. He only accompanied his wife and wasn't expected to take any form of employment as the spouse of a diplomat. He was so angry about the inversion of roles! He saw himself as a house husband and didn't like the idea that his wife was the bread winner. She never returned home from her official duties before eleven o'clock at night. She often went on consular visits to other cities in Italy and spent days before coming back. Then she represented the High Commission in local community programmes during the weekends. I was often left alone in their big home with this man who turned me into his sex slave. He blackmailed me, saying he'd tell my Madame that I was the one making advances at him. He knew she wouldn't believe me, and I had no other choice than to accommodate him. I worked for them for four long years. I should have graduated from the university by now if I'd remained in *Naija*. Now, after these four years my Madame got posted to South Africa. To my great surprise, she refused to take me along. She said she'd done enough for me and that I was big enough to fend for myself. I refused to stand and work on the streets. I've always been fascinated by the world of the internet and social networking, I'm smart, so I do my own thing on my own terms and conditions."

Joy remained speechless after hearing her story. They had both been trafficked and deceived by those they trusted most. Unlike her, she owed money which had to be paid back in due course. She had also been made to take an oath binding her to repayment. She had had to pay dearly with the life of her father. Her mother still lived under the constant threat of her sister, Comfort. She did not know what was to happen next. Her mother had told her never to return and that she would be able to stand up to her sister. Charity had stated clearly that she did not want to work on the streets. This aroused Joy's curiosity. She had said she did her own thing on her own terms and conditions. Joy could not make any sense of these words and wanted to investigate further.

"So what job do you do?"

"Job? There're no jobs in this country except the one you create for yourself. It depends on how you decide to run your business and what name you want to give yourself."

"I still don't get it."

"First things first. Your first worry for now should not be a job. You have a roof over your head, and we can share this place for now. That reminds me, we should be returning to the *Avvocato* within the next two weeks. Until then it's risky and inadvisable for you to go out alone. You're lucky you've not been questioned or picked up already. That would further weaken your case, so I advise you to lie low for now until your application slip gets to you."

"I'm worried about his fee. He didn't specify how much he was charging for his service. He got me really worried, and if I owe him, I'd want to know how much at least."

"Don't worry about him. The important thing is that he'll surely do what he promised. Leave the payment part of it to me."

"What exactly do you mean? Are you going to pay for me?"

"That brings me back to the job I do. The *Avvocato* is one of my clients. My job is simply to do what it takes to make good money, including sleeping with my clients or even blackmailing them. You see, the *Avvocato* would do anything to protect his secret from his wife. He dreads being exposed and excommunicated from the Roman Catholic Church. Guess who else is on my client list? You'll never be able to guess even if I give you your entire life to do so."

"Then just go ahead and tell me. Is he someone I should know?"

"Yes, he is the almighty and infallible Consular Officer himself. Forget about all his long preaching and big grammar. He's a pretender, a hypocrite like many others in the same position. His case is exactly the opposite of my Madame who works in the same High Commission. His wife's bored too, staying all day at home just like my Madame's husband. Her children are all grown up and are in different universities around Europe, so the poor woman is left alone at home most of the time, except on the very few occasions when she's required to accompany her husband on official duties. You know women are not like men. She soon found ways of keeping herself busy. She's involved in a private business, as she can't take up any official job just like my Madame's husband. She travels often to Dubai to buy different products which she takes to *Naija* for distribution. She's hardly ever at home. Her husband has found a way of keeping himself busy by engaging my services. He takes me right into his home and afterwards behaves as if girls like us are a disgrace to our country, when all of them patronise our business. They're all corrupt. They know they won't survive without us. They need us, with or without their wives."

Joy was not even minimally shocked by her revelations. She only reminded her of Mercy. Mercy had told her in Torino that there was nothing like prostitution, that everything had to do with being professional and how one is presented and at what level and profile one operated. Charity had just confirmed this. She worked as a prostitute but had a different approach and profile of her business, which did not make it look like what it really was.

"Now tell me, how does your business work?"

"I have very exclusive and very few clients, I choose those who are generous and have a secret to hide. I also target old people with pension money. Those men are ready to pay anything to get a piece of the action. So lesson number one is to target your client group. Some of our girls are too greedy and unwise. They think they'll make more money when they sleep with more men, but sometimes you can make more money sleeping with one man or not sleeping with any at all. It depends on how smart you are."

"And lesson number two?"

"After targeting your clients—that's identifying your market and answering the question 'who?'—you'll need to go on to phase two and answer the question 'how?' That's how you go about it and where you source your information from. This is the age of technology, and it works for me. See, all you need is a smartphone. You'll learn how to use it to create your client profile and design how you want to run your business. It's entirely up to you. If you need some help to start, there are business centres where they can link you up with prospective clients. I can even give you the link to some of my clients who might want to try something new. I'm here to help you, and before you know it, you're made."

Joy was beginning to like the whole idea. There was still one last lesson, and Charity did not forget to mention it. "You'll need to go to a Living Bible Church."

"Church? Did I hear you right? What has church got to do with it?"

"You'll need to belong to a church for two reasons. First for cover-up, so that no one really knows what you're doing. No born-again Christian would do the kind of job we do, but that's life for you. The second reason why you need to go to church is that you really need God to be on your side. Don't forget, I said Living Bible Church, not Catholic or Anglican where you go and nobody sees you. You need the kind of church where you'll be visible."

Although she would still have to work as a prostitute, Joy found peace and consolation in the fact that she was not required to work in the cold streets, expose herself to the harsh and unfriendly winter weather, or be on the nervous lookout for any surprise police raid. She could feel herself free again, as a person capable of making her own choices and decisions. If she had her way, she would rather choose not to go this road at all. As things stood, she was content at least with the fact that she could run her business herself and determine who she allowed to touch her body, for how much, and for how long. Most importantly, she would get to keep all the money for herself. She could begin to dream again and look towards the future with confidence. She had three long years in front of her. These would be more than enough for her to pull deals that were good enough to say goodbye for the last time to the nightmare of the reality of Europe and all its empty promises.

For the next two weeks Joy spent her time building what was to become her one-woman business enterprise, a limited liability company providing diversified services in the field of human relations and resources. She carefully thought and spelt out her client group and defined both limits and off limits of business transactions. To seal the deal, she did not forget Charity's recommendation. She made a vow to God and called on his divine protection and mercy. She knew her prayers did not fall on deaf ears and that he was with her even in her state of slavery and sinfulness. She knew she would be delivered at the right time, three years on, and then she would do only the right thing for the rest of her life.

"Double good news, sis! I told you it's going to work out! I've just picked up your asylum application slip from the *Avvocato*. Here it is."

Charity handed her the fifth of an A4 sheet with the name Joy Kamara on it. Joy was thunderstruck. She could not understand why such an insignificant piece of paper would carry all the importance it was meant to stand for. She had just been handed a licence that would permit her to remain without harassment for the next three years or more. That paper not only gave her the reason to linger on but also took away her real identity and nationality.

"You should be the happiest person on earth with that paper you're holding. You must keep it safe and carry it with you at all times. If you misplace it, then that's the end."

"It's not that I'm not happy. You know how it feels when you finally get what you think is impossible? It feels like a dream and you simply don't believe it. Thanks. That reminds me, what about the second good news?"

"It's about your first client. He's Salvatore. He'll pick you up today at eight o'clock."

# Chapter Fourteen

Salvatore was officially enrolled as an engineering student in the university. He hated the subject with a passion. He also hated having to fulfil the frustrated dream of his father to become the only engineer in the family. His real passion was for society, social interactions, and culture. He was particularly fascinated by the attitude of his culture towards women. He only needed to look at himself as he grew up in what was apparently a "normal" and "happy" family to see the true picture of his society as a global village. Right from a very tender age, he enjoyed the benefits of a paternalistic society and the stereotyping of women to their detriment.

His father, Michele, was his model as a man and father. He worked so hard to ensure that his family lacked nothing, but he had a dark side to his seemingly good attributes as an ideal father and an exceptional husband. He abused his wife Maria both verbally and physically. She lived under the tyranny of a man who was more of a master than a husband. Salvatore often heard his mother sob at nights and had wondered why she never left him or even went to the police.

"Where do I go? A mother's place is always with her children in her husband's home. A good mother must never abandon her family, no matter what happens," she often said to her son. He knew that his mother was the product of a culture of silence. What he did not know was that she was coping with much more than an abusive husband who had taken away every sense of dignity and femininity from her. For many years she had known and lived with the shocking discovery that her husband had another family and other mistresses too. She dreaded the day that her son would come to discover who his adorable and respectable father really was. Her entire life was geared towards keeping this secret from seeing the light of the day. She had to stay to keep her family intact and to protect her son and his inheritance and prevent his other women from making legitimate claims on it.

Although Salvatore was sympathetic towards the plight of his mother, the outside world did not show him a different picture of the deplorable violence against women. The media constantly highlighted episodes of femicide of both Italian and foreign women as a daily occurrence, with women killed, buried alive, set ablaze, strangled, poisoned, or shot by husbands, partners, boyfriends, exes, or unidentified clients. These victims of *feminicidio* were only guilty of resistance, rebellion, or simply the affirmation and fierce defence of their individuality as persons, irrespective of whether they were named or shamed by the same men, who at one point or the other in their lives stood for all they ever wanted or desired. More often than not, their apparently unexpected demise was not surprising. They had cried for help from their homes, which had become the most unsafe and dangerous place for them to be. They had visited police stations and *carabinieri,* who simply sent them back to their future killers. In twelve years, 2,200 women had been murdered, an average of 171 a year and one every two days, yet the former Catholic parish priest of *San Terenzo di Lerici* sentenced them to a "healthy self-criticism" in the form of *mea culpa,* while the judges frequently acquitted the perpetrators, making reference to the "crime of passion", a modern day re-visitation of honour killings. Compared to the tragic and untimely end of these women, Salvatore felt that the position of his mother was probably the better option as a true replica of the silence of the lambs.

Salvatore was simply a child of his age and time. At thirty, he was everything most Italians of his age were: narcissistic, patriarchal, and a male chauvinist. He grew up with the disenchanted and unquestioned habits of sexually harassing women with unequivocal looks and passing chauvinistic comments with impunity. "*Che bella bisteccona!*" he often said to young women, comparing them to an appetising and mouth-watering chunk of steak. He still lived under the same roof with both parents like most Italians of his age, expecting their not-too-imminent death in order to inherit their property.

His father had imposed two conditions which he must meet if he wanted to enter into his legitimate inheritance as his only son. He had to graduate from the university as an engineer and bear him a grandson. Salvatore knew that it was better and easier for him to meet these conditions than to try to be a man of his own. He did not want to join the unending queue of unemployment or leave his country for greener pastures as many had done in recent times. As far as graduating as an engineer was concerned, he knew he had all the time in the world, as his father had not imposed any time limit on him. "Before I die" was what he said, and this could easily be translated to mean *ad infinituum*. The university too was not in a hurry to see him graduate. The operative *fuori corso* system allowed him to remain a student for an indefinite period, as long as he sat some minimally required exams each year.

Although he was engaged to Bianca, a third-year medical student at the same university, he could not explain his inordinate desire to explore the unusual flavours of pay-as-you-go sex. His innate yet undiagnosed racism was the reason for his passion and desire for black-skinned girls. He could pay them and then use, abuse, and humiliate them as a way of establishing his supremacy. For a long time he had contemplated paying a visit to the girls on the sidewalk.

He was also a true son of his father and had mastered the rules of the game. His father had told him that real crime lay not in its being committed but in its being discovered, that no one was a criminal until he was caught, and that any uncaught criminal was no criminal at all, except those who were stupid enough to bite the bait. His friends too had told him about how he could hook up with girls online without necessarily exposing himself as a consumer of this rare and prohibited commodity. He had been looking for this perfect solution.

At a quarter to eight he pulled up his car at the agreed spot and waited for the arrival of his sex date. He felt like it was his first day in elementary school. His date finally arrived punctually and climbed into the front seat of his car. He could not believe the vision that had just appeared right next to him. She was everything but the person he had expected to meet. She was gorgeous, stunning, angelic, bewitching, and delightfully charming.

Joy's own expectations had also not turned out exactly the way she had expected. She had looked forward to another example of the kind of men she had previously met: old, shabby, pot-bellied, ugly, and unsightly with rude and impolite characters, nasty men with unpleasant smells who sometimes turned up in labourer's clothes. What was now before her was a cute, appealing, good-looking, smartly dressed young man. In a moment she quickly forgot the original point of arranged meeting. She had just met her Prince Charming who reciprocated her every excitement and pleasant surprise.

Salvatore was speechless. This was definitely more than he had bargained for. He was convinced that she could not in any way have been a prostitute. He was sure there was a mix up somewhere along the line, and he was bent on finding out. He had to change his plan for the evening. He took her to a café in the *laurentina* area where they could have an initial chat.

"My name is Salvatore," he managed to say in a voice that uncovered his embarrassment and shame.

"I'm Joy." She was not in any better situation than he was.

After they finally broke the ice, he was very curious to know more about the young woman who had changed his entire life even without knowing it. He had never believed that women could be forced into prostitution. His father always told him that all women were prostitutes and that survival prostitution was a job like every other, but the woman before him did not appear to fit this pattern. Even without her uttering a word about her odyssey, he knew she had been trafficked and that whatever she did or was about to do was not a decision taken in complete freedom.

They chatted for the rest of the evening. Towards eleven-thirty they left as the café was getting ready to close at midnight. He accompanied her back to her flat and gave her a 100 euros note. He was surprised that she ignored his offer and simply said goodnight as she alighted from the car and galloped like a gazelle into the dark. This left him in total confusion. Had he just been with a lady of the night? His friends had boasted about their encounters, especially their first time, and he had been eagerly looking forward to sharing his experience with them over a glass of house red wine the next evening, but his twist with this mysterious girl was something he could never share with anyone, not even his most intimate friends. They would laugh at him and find it impossible to believe that he found an angel when he intentionally went in search of one of the daughters of Jezebel.

Charity could not wait to hear of the outcome of her appointment the evening before. It made her happy to know that she was a good life coach and that her instructions had been fruitfully employed.

"Let's see your take-home for your first job. How much is it?"

"Nothing."

"What do you mean by nothing? Do you mean to tell me that you worked for free or that he refused to pay you? Don't you know the importance of the first client in business, that if the first one doesn't pay, it spoils your luck for the rest?"

"I didn't work for free. I didn't even work at all. He gave me a 100 euros but I refused to take it."

"How stupid can you be? What do you mean you didn't work? You spent close to four hours with him. He should pay you for your time. Time is money. Don't you understand? By the way, why didn't you collect the money he offered you?"

"I think I'm in love with him. He's not that kind of guy."

"What kind of guy? Can't you remember who he was looking for when he contacted us? It's pure business, and love's got nothing to do with it. You really need to learn fast. Money's the reason you're here. You must make sure you're paid for your services before anything else, and please forget that thing you call love. An *Italo* can't ever love a black woman, especially one he meets in the situation he met you. Save your love for when you've made enough money. Then you can buy anything, including love and a good husband."

Joy paid no attention at all to her sermon. She knew what she felt for him. She had never felt that way before for anyone, not even for Pastor Joshua, the first and only man who truly loved her. She was convinced that destiny was at work here and that her encounter with Salvatore, no matter the circumstances, was not in any way casual. For the first time the whole ordeal of her travel and transit started to make sense to her. She had travelled all the way, risked her life, lost a kidney and even her father in exchange for finding the love of her life in a foreign land. And it was worth every bit of the sacrifice she had made. She was happy that she did not settle for the offer of a loveless marriage with Mimmo. Now she could have love too, probably in addition to all the benefits that accompanied being married to an Italian.

Over the next two months Salvatore's visits became an everyday routine. Against the advice of Charity, she had refused to attend other appointments. She was certain that things would work in her favour and that a healthy relationship with Salvatore was all that was required. She loved him too. Her love justified whatever they did together. It wiped away every feeling of sinfulness and removed every sense of guilt. She gave herself freely and unconditionally to him. It was the most natural thing for her. It felt right, unlike the other times when men took advantage of her and made her feel worthless and dirty. The money they paid in exchange was never enough to make her feel clean.

One evening Salvatore took her to the same café they had been to on their first date. Joy was sure that he had something really important to tell her. She hoped it was exactly the same thing she had been looking forward to with all eagerness.

"I brought you here today because I really want to discuss a business deal with you."

"Business?" she thought to herself. She had been expecting him to talk of love or their two-month relationship and its logical way forward.

"I know you're wondering why I'm talking about business. Everything in life is about business, so it's good for you to know this right from the start so that you know exactly what you're getting yourself into. Okay, I know your situation. I want to help you by marrying you."

He had been honest enough to speak about business at the start of their conversation. It did not come as a surprise to her that his proposal carried no romantic undertone. He had carefully chosen to use the word "help" when she had expected him to confess endless love. She appreciated his sincerity and wanted to know what he expected in return for the favour of marrying her.

"You'll bear me a child."

"A child?"

"Yes, a child, but that's not the main thing. It has to be before I marry you."

She questioned whether things would ever be normal for her. Why did he insist on having a child before marriage and not the other way round as is usually the practice? She had always believed in doing things in the right order, but reality always played a fast one on her. "So you won't marry me unless I have a baby for you?"

"That's why I spoke about business. You do something for me, and I do something for you. My dad wants me to have a child before I inherit his property. He said nothing about marriage, so he's fine with me having his grandchild without marrying. This last bit is what I'm doing to help you. I don't need to be married, but you do. If you'd gone to school a little bit more you'd come across the definition of marriage as a 'social contract'."

She knew it was not the time to be sentimental. Whatever the case, there was still a valid marriage proposal awaiting a response, a response that would change her story for the better. She did not want to wait any further. She could never get a better deal even if she lived for the next fifty years. This was that one big occasion she had waited for. Then again, a child born on Italian soil would give her enough reasons to obtain a legal right of abode as a mother. The marriage was a value-added asset to an already settled situation of permanent residence. She could not ask or desire anything more.

"What about your parents? What will they say? Will they like me?"

"This's Italy. You're getting married to me, not to my entire family like you do in Africa. If you want to meet them, I can arrange a meeting in four weeks' time, that is, when I have confirmation that you're pregnant. *Andiamo!* Let's go! We've got a job to do!"

Joy shared the good news with Charity when she returned home late that evening. To her greatest surprise, Charity did not share her enthusiasm. She warned her unsympathetically against the imminent danger that she was too blinded by love to see. She tried to get her to refocus and concentrate on her newly launched business. Make enough money and leave the country before the rejection of her political asylum as a Liberian became official. She relied heavily on the fact that she had lived longer in Italy and knew the country and people better. As much as she tried, none of her arguments was able to change Joy's mind about her decision. On her part, Joy could not understand why her only friend was making so much effort to dissuade her. She felt she was not the friend she had claimed to be and was only being unreasonably jealous of her newfound fortune.

Four weeks later Salvatore brought Joy to his parents in their home in *via oderisi da gubbio*. The visit was both a remake and reversal of the film *Guess Who's Coming to Dinner?* with Sidney Poitier. Maria, Salvatore's mother, could not hide her disgust and disappointment at her only son as she dragged him to the privacy of her room. She had never left Italy and, like Lucia the old nun, she still nurtured barbaric ideas about Africans. She was a traditional woman and understood perfectly well what it meant for her son to bring a girl home to his parents. She had always looked forward to a day like this. Salvatore had previously brought home Bianca but had only introduced her as a friend. Almost three years later, nothing more had followed. It seemed to be one of those long engagements that were never destined to end in marriage. Ever since then, Maria had been watching and waiting for her son to do the right thing. Now that he had finally done so, he had only succeeded in opening a can of worms.

"*Mai!* Never!" She hurled the words at him.

"*Mamma*, it's not as you think." He tried to calm her down and bring her to reason as she paced up and down the room, muttering incantations in the Sicilian dialect. "*E' inutile*. It's no use," he continued. "She's already pregnant and I've married her."

Maria was not sure she had heard her son correctly. If she had, she was unsure whether she understood his words. They simply fell into one ear and out of the other as if they were never said or intended to be heard. She struggled to balance herself as she sat on the nearby bed. Salvatore did all he could to reassure her, pleading with her to trust him. Mother and son had been accomplices in the past. She had always protected her son and excused his excesses. This was definitely one of those exceptional cases that could lead her as an authentic *siciliana* to disown him as a son as she had threatened to do in the past. But he was still his only beloved son, the one she had always justified even when he was in the wrong. "*Tutto a posto*. It's all right," she had often assured him. Now was the time to prove it.

Meanwhile his father, Michele was in the *soggiorno*, asking his surprise daughter in-law a myriad of questions. His weakness was women. He was always fascinated and bewitched by anything in skirts. His philosophy differed significantly from that of his wife. Women for him were simply women. Their only purpose was to meet the sexual needs of men and have children. He had no problems as long as they met both requirements, be they black, yellow, or white. The girl before him had just met one of his criteria, the more important one at that.

Michele had always held divergent views from his son about almost everything. He often found himself alone, while his wife and son held similar opinions. But on this most important issue he had to agree with his son for the first time, if only to spite his wife and make her feel like a loser in a game that was yet to start.

"*Bravo, figliolo!* Well done, son!" He was beside himself with exhilaration. Salvatore had never seen his father this happy since the day of his first communion. He knew he had won his heart once and for all.

At long last.

# Epilogue

Two years after the birth of Francesco, Joy was living with Salvatore and his parents, Maria and Michele. She had married Salvatore for love, but the main reason was to remain legally in Italy. She could not go back to Nigeria. She feared being re-trafficked to another part of Europe. She had not paid back the 80,000 euros she still owed Comfort. Previously, she had hoped that she would think of that once she had permanent residence in Italy, but things took a drastic turn after she met, fell in love and married Salvatore. She had found a second home in Italy and as long as she remained there, she was safe. Her mother had assured her of her ability to handle her own sister Comfort. She had done her worst by causing the death of her husband, who by the way was a burden to her. Without knowing it, Comfort had saved Joy's life and given her a reason to be the woman she had always wanted to be.

Maria, Salvatore's mother, was not in any way placated by the arrival of a grandson. This foreign woman in one single act had taken away the two most important men in her life. That she added a third was not important to her. She was bent on taking back what had been stolen from her and she made that her reason to be. She found fault and complained about anything Joy did. She took pleasure in humiliating her lack of proper upbringing and grooming. She could not even boil an egg, when real Italian women were expected to do everything that pleased the husband, including not just preparing his own favourite dish but the favourite dishes of the nation as well, such as *lasagne*. She was also expected to be able to entertain guests, especially at traditional, cultural, and religious celebrations such as Christmas and prepare the traditional end of year meals like *salsiccie* and *lenticchie*. Joy could not even prepare a simple Italian meal like boiling pasta, especially spaghetti, without making it look like worms.

Maria found it particularly vexing that Joy had not been properly prepared to embark on the journey of motherhood. She could not properly care for her son Francesco. She could not sing traditional *nina nana* or other bedside songs or stories in a language she was yet to understand herself. She particularly hated taking him to the park and just watching him play for hours. It was as much a waste of time as the time she spent with the nuns learning the skills she would never need even once in her entire life.

Joy's greatest challenge was having to ask for money. Salvatore's family gave her everything she needed except financial independence. She hated asking for money, especially to send home to her poor mother and siblings. Michele, her father-in-law, was smart enough to identify this need and exploit the opportunity it presented. He was ready to give her any amount of money she needed just for the asking, but on his terms and conditions. Joy found herself being prostituted in her own matrimonial home.

When she could no longer bear the humiliations of Maria, the nonchalance of her husband Salvatore, and the continuous lust and rape of Michele, she decided to seek a way of exit, only to discover the greatest shock of her life.

Salvatore confessed that their marriage was a fake one. He was never cut out for marriage. He had only wanted a child in order to secure his inheritance. What was more? He had always maintained his relationship with Bianca. She loved him so much but was not ready to spoil her figure with the demands of maternity just to please a man. "Find a surrogate and I'll be the perfect wife and mother," she had suggested. Joy was the much-desired anchor mother she needed in order to have her cake and eat it too.

Joy could not believe that she was right back where she started. The only difference now was her son Francesco. Surely she would have some rights over him as a mother since the marriage to his father had been null and void?

She contacted Avvocato Carpisa, and the news she received was even more appalling. He had been registered at birth as *M.Ignota,* which literarily stood for an unknown mother or a prostitute.

Joy still had two years to wait before the outcome of her application for political asylum as a Liberian with the name Joy Kamara. Her only choice was to return to the most ancient business in the world, the one for which she was brought to Italy. It was indeed a return to the future and to destiny.

Joy Osaro, *aka* Joy Kamara, was the embodiment of the joy that was never meant to be. She was the unfulfilled dream and aspiration of the woman without dignity, identity, or nationality. She was the sound of silence that was too loud to be heard.

# GLOSSARY

Arrivederci: (Italian) Goodbye

Ascolta: (Italian) Listen

Ashawo: (Slang, Nigerian) Prostitute

ATM: Automatic Teller machine

Avvocato: (Italian) Lawyer

Badante; (Italian) Carer, Caregiver

Basta: (Italian) Enough

Boko Haram: An extremist Islamic group in Nigeria

Calma: (Italian) Calm down

Caritas: A Catholic charity

Chador: Cloth or scarf used by Muslim woman to wrap around the body except the face.

Che bella bisteccona: (Italian) What a beautiful chunk of steak

Che tragedia: (Italian) What a tragedy

Comune: (Italian) City council

Collegio: (Italian) College

Condominio: (Italian) Condominium

Femminicidio: (Italian) femicide

Gratuito patroncinio: (Italian) Free legal aid

Grazie, Signora" (Italian) Thank you, Madame

Italo: (Informal, Nigerian) Italy, Italian

Italos: (Informal, Nigerian) Italians

Jambite: (Slang, Nigerian) One who gains admission to the university through JAMB (Joint Admission and matriculation Board), a newcomer or fresher

Jihab: Cloth or scarf used by Muslim woman to cover the face except the eyes

Keke Napep: A tricycle used in the Nigerian transportation system

Kpali: (Informal, Slang) Passport

Naija: (Informal) Nigeria or Nigerian

Naira: Nigerian currency

Nettezza Urbana: (Italian) Garbage tax

Ogbalegbe : (Bini language, Nigerian) A police officer, member of the armed forces, law enforcement agent

Permesso di soggiorno: (Italian) Foreigner's stay or residence permit

Questura: (Italian) Police Headquarters

Shine your eye: (Nigerian, Slang)

Siciliana: (Italian) A woman from Sicily

Soggiorno: (Italian) Living Room

Suor/Suora: (Italian) Nun, Reverend Sister

# About the Author

Pauline Aweto holds a PhD from the Pontifical Salesian University, Rome, Italy. She has written extensively and contributed to research and publications on Gender, including "North African Feminism" in the Routledge International Encyclopaedia of Women: Global Women's Issues and Knowledge (2000). She is also the author of the books, Wartime Rape: African Values at Crossroads (2010) and The Changing Lanscape of Christianity in Africa (2012).

She has been actively involved in the socio cultural integration of migrants, especially of African women in Italy, She was an invited lecturer to the Third University of Rome, Romatre and was for four years a permanent member of the European Project: Equity and Difference across and within European Countries, Training for a Culture of Difference.

She was also a Consultant with the International Organisation for Migration (IOM/OIM) within the Programme of the Assisted Voluntary Return and Reintegration of the Victims of Human Trafficking for Sexual Exploitation.

Currently, she is a part time lecturer in the United Kingdom and an Independent Consultant to Non-Governmental Organisations working for the reintegration of trafficked women in Italy.

## Book Teaser

A compelling story of conflict between the forces of faith and fate. Joy's greatest nightmare became reality when she came face to face with the tragic lies, crime and deceit behind the veil of the empty promises of a better life in Europe. Exactly how far is she ready to defy her plight and dare to be different? Will she make up her mind, for the last time, to embrace what had timelessly been revealed as her true destiny from which she could no longer run away?

## Endorsement

This is a story that needs to be told. It is deeply moving and challenging, and portrays the terrible plight of a trafficked woman".

Antonia Stampalija

Printed in Great Britain
by Amazon